# HOW TO HOMESCHOOL MATH
### – Even if you Hate Fractions!!

Copyright © 2011 By Robin Padron
All Rights Reserved.

Isbn-10: 146367354X
Ean-13: 9781463673543

# HOW TO HOMESCHOOL MATH
## – Even if you Hate Fractions!!

Robin Padron

*This book is dedicated*

*To Alex and Scott,*

*Who have taught me way more*

*Than I can ever hope*

*To teach them!*

# TABLE OF CONTENTS

Introduction ........................................... ix

**Chapter 1: The Full-Contact Approach** ................. 1
In which I define the Full-Contact approach and compare it to the traditional approach.

**Chapter 2: Arithmetic and Pre-Algebra**.............. 23
In which I discuss the nuts and bolts of how to teach math at this stage.

**Chapter 3: Common Pitfalls** ....................... 43
In which I discuss the common challenges homeschooling families face.

**Chapter 4: Algebra 1 and Geometry** ................. 59
In which I present an in-depth description of these classical courses, as well as effective strategies for teaching them.

**Chapter 5: Math Tutoring** ......................... 79
In which I discuss how to get the most out of a tutor. What works, what doesn't, when to use one and when not to bother.

## Chapter 6: Algebra 2, Pre-Calculus and Calculus          89
In which I present an in-depth description of these classical courses, as well as effective strategies for teaching them.

## Chapter 7: Incentives          101
In which I discuss various incentives for math students that work and don't work.

## Chapter 8: Hope & Motivation          117
In which I discuss how to turn around an unwilling student, and some motivation for parents.

## Appendix: The List of Topics          135
In which I outline all the major math topics in the most effective order of instruction.

# INTRODUCTION

I'm a typical homeschooling mom – raising my kids, putting up with a constantly messy and chaotic home, opinionated in-laws, and the periodic anxiety of wondering if this was all a big mistake. Life often feels too busy and too disorganized, but then I have those moments of joy, and I am reassured that homeschooling is absolutely the right choice for me and my family.

Homeschooling was actually kind of thrust upon me when my oldest son Alex was in 5$^{th}$ grade. We live in a lovely, small town in Connecticut, and we were happy enough with our local elementary school. OK, the kids didn't learn much, but they had fun with all their friends, and I had no major complaints.

That year Alex came down with an obscure stomach virus, which periodically gave him debilitating stomachaches. He was perfectly fine in between episodes, but he missed about two days of school each week, and it was hard for him to keep up with projects and homework. I had always loved the idea of homeschooling, and it didn't seem like Alex was learning much that year anyway, so when my doctor told me that Alex might stay sick *indefinitely*, I decided to start homeschooling him.

I jumped right into the homeschool lifestyle, joining co-ops and making friends and plans. We got our schoolwork done in just an hour or two, then got busy with wilderness school, soccer and all sorts of other things that Alex could simply miss when he got sick. Homeschooling looked like so much fun that Alex's younger brother, Scott, decided to start homeschooling too.

Like many of you, I myself had gone to school. I got A's in math, but I can tell you honestly, I learned nothing. I think I was a good test taker. I was good at the mechanics, and I could spit back what was put in front of me – but really, I had no idea what any of it *meant*. Nor did I really care! I was grade-focused, and it never occurred to me that my subjects in school were anything to really think deeply or care about. It all seemed incredibly meaningless. I wish that were not true, but there it is.

Alex has always been a "math eager" kid, and when we started homeschooling, he was excited to do more advanced math than he had been getting at school. He was a little tired of getting pages of three-digit multiplications to do as a "reward" for having finished his work quickly. Because he was only in $5^{th}$ grade, and I was supposedly "good at math," I felt pretty confident about this.

However, I have to say, that I had to re-learn absolutely everything! Seriously. I couldn't remember how to add two fractions! Let alone how to explain it.

So I cracked the books and set out to re-learn my math. It was *work*, no doubt, but it was worth it. I have stayed one step ahead of Alex all the way through AP Calculus, and it has been an incredible learning experience for me. I re-learned my math with the purpose of teaching it to my children, and that made it so much more meaningful and interesting. I had to really *think* about it now, in order to

## Introduction

explain it. No longer could I just go through the motions, as I had for years in school.

I was instantly captivated. For me it started with explaining what dividing by a fraction means. I can honestly say that I had never really thought about it before. I must have done this in school, I'm sure, but really thought about it? No, never.

I had the enthusiasm that any "newbie" has. I was excited about math, and excited about teaching it. Over time I started teaching math courses at my homeschool co-ops. That has blossomed into a busy private math-tutoring business. I now tutor and teach classes to both school-kids and homeschoolers, on everything from Arithmetic to AP Calculus.

This book is based on my years of experience teaching not only my own boys, but also many other homeschoolers and school-children. I have been lucky enough to really get to know many of the parents, and this has given me great insight into what works and what doesn't.

Both of my boys are years "ahead" in math. That is nice, but honestly not super important to me. That they like math and feel confident with it – now <u>that</u> is important to me. I am also happy to report that Alex is totally recovered.

This is *not* a book on "How to get your gifted child to the math Olympiads." This is a book for *regular* families, with *regular* kids, who want to give their kids a good, solid mathematical foundation and skills that they can be proud of and take into the future with them. It is a set of guidelines, a philosophy of teaching math, an attitude and an approach that any family seeking to homeschool math can benefit from.

This book will actually <u>not</u> teach any math. No fractions! No long division! There are many excellent textbooks out there that will help you with that. This is a book about what you <u>do</u> with the textbook. The way you interact with your child is *so* much more important than which particular curriculum you choose. This book is full of concrete suggestions that will help you finally give your kids the skills they need, without making them "hate math."

Hopefully you will find some ideas in these pages that lead you to a more joyful and productive homeschool math experience.

# CHAPTER ONE
## FULL-CONTACT MATH

I used to love reading stories to my kids when they were little. All those evenings snuggled up in a blanket, sharing a story are now precious memories. For years I read to them every night, and very often it was the most relaxing and special time of my day.

Almost all of us parents read stories to our children when they are young. Everywhere we go we hear exhortations to read to our kids. Public service announcements abound, springing themselves upon us at regular intervals. On the radio: Read to Your Kids! During the 11 o'clock news: Read to Your Kids! In the parenting books and magazines: Read to Your Kids! Society is all over us, urging us to read to our kids. Of course, we know that reading to our children makes them Adults who Love to Read, and this is what we hope for them.

We all love our kids. We want the best for them, so we *do* read to them – all the time. Most of us have bedtime story time, and many have our own family story times and traditions. We spend a small fortune on toddler books. We even buy floaty books for the bathtub! We pack up the car and drive to town for storytime at the library. This is what we do. No matter how tired or busy we may be, we make time for stories!

And, by and large, our kids seem to be turning out to be young men and women who do enjoy reading. I think that most of us would agree that reading to our kids does, in fact, work.

But why? Is it the books themselves that have some kind of inspirational magic? Would it be equally as effective if we just had books "available" to them, and never actually sat down and read out loud to them? Would simply putting an iPod on the kids each day and playing an audiobook while we vacuum in the other room work just as well?

No way!

When we read to our kids, not only are they hearing new words and stories that spark their imaginations, but they are also, more importantly, <u>bonding with us</u>. Story time is precious; a time when they have our undivided time and attention. We put all other things aside, and show them *with our actions* that they, and reading, are the most important things in our world. Even if just for a few minutes, you, they and the book are all that matters.

While the stories themselves are obviously enjoyable, it is our undivided and loving parental attention that is associated with reading in their minds. In fact, many kids will still join in family storytime, snuggled up and cozy, even if they really don't care for the story that their sibling happened to pick that night. They stay and listen anyway. It is as if we are brainwashing them in a good way: We are constantly associating reading with a mother's or father's love. Pretty powerful stuff. People crave connectedness, children especially, and most of us parents spend at least the first ten years of our kids' lives consciously and deliberately associating reading with human, familial, parental connectedness. No wonder this stuff works!

*Chapter One: Full-Contact Math*

And of course, it is not just reading with which this approach works. Consider the woman who loves fly-fishing because her father took her every Sunday and spent the entire morning lovingly, patiently and joyfully sharing the experience with her. Think of the musical director whose passion for music was inspired by his mother who spent hours, days, weeks, years sharing her love of music with her son.

These stories do not surprise us. We all know that this is how it works. Kids often love what we love; do what we do; are excited about things that excite us. As loving and involved homeschooling parents, we all read to our kids all the time. We also spend lots of time doing other activities with them. We watch history movies together, play interesting games together. Maybe we discuss religion or politics at the dinner table. We cheer at their sports games and clap at their recitals. Each one of these activities takes up a parent's valuable time, which kids of any age know is limited and precious. When we do these activities with our children we are showing, with our actions, our time and our pocketbooks that they are important.

But when it comes to math – with math it's a whole different story! Maybe we do start out early with lots of interaction: counting yellow duckies and the like, but pretty soon it is: "Take these exercises, go off into solitary confinement and do them. Then come back and I'll tell you what you did wrong."

After years of story time, reading represents connection, love and warmth. Math, on the other hand, starts to represent banishment, social isolation and criticism! We show our kids that math is not something enjoyable or interesting, by not enjoying it or being interested in it ourselves. We will read stories with them, bake cupcakes with them, watch history movies with them, even do science experiments with them, but do math together? No way!

We all know that the United States lags behind other nations in math. We know that math skills are vital to our kids' succeeding in today's global economy, yet our actions belie these facts. We may be saying math is important, but we are *demonstrating* that it is not.

Why? Why do we approach teaching math so differently than other subjects? This is a question that has been perplexing me for years: What causes so many of us parents to behave so differently with math than with almost everything else we want our kids to learn and enjoy?

## Full-Contact Math

Imagine snuggling up with your children to watch a funny math video, or hanging their math problems proudly up on the fridge. Envision your family talking about math around the dinner table, or your kid saying "Let's do math!" and having that mean the same as "Let's read a story!" What if math was something you did and enjoyed together?

Maybe it sounds ridiculous and fantastical at best, and seriously unpleasant at worst, but this is what it's like in my home. Because I have two boys, I like to call it "Full-Contact Math." Full-Contact math involves you, the parent, being involved in *each and every little bit of math* you expect your kids to do, until they are good, ready, willing and able to happily take off on their own. It is showing them – with your actions, your precious *time* and *attention*, that math is important, interesting, and worthwhile.

Full-Contact math is a commitment to spend "math time" together, which is a fundamental shift in the way most of us think about teaching our kids math.

## Chapter One: Full-Contact Math

Before you shut this book in disgust, let me say that you do *not* have to be good at math, or even *like* math to take it "Full-Contact." Throughout this book I will provide many concrete suggestions that any family can follow and benefit from. For now, let it suffice that, if you have graduated high school, then you can definitely do this!

I also promise you that you can do this enthusiastically! As parents we are masters of "exaggerated enthusiasm." We talk endlessly and enthusiastically about Barbies, Polly-Pockets, ponies and warships. That takes some serious devotion! You will be happy to know that all that time spent "Ooohing" and "Aahing" about spiders and worms, honing your enthusiasm skills, will again be put to good use!

I have been teaching my own kids math Full-Contact for years. I know from personal experience that 10 minutes of math time with me and my undivided attention is far more productive for my kids than an hour spent doing exercises off on their own. I firmly believe in the idea of '"less time, more connection" as an effective way to teach math.

I actually thought that *all* homeschool families did it this way. It was only when I started tutoring other homeschool kids that I began to understand how rare it is, even in our high-contact homeschool world.

Alex came out of school when he was in 5$^{th}$ grade. Math was Alex's favorite subject even then, and all reports were that he was "good" at it. So I knew right away that if I were going to homeschool him, I'd have to get right on top of this math thing.

Since he had just started homeschooling, we were not yet entrenched with a million homeschool activities, and our days seemed long and empty until afternoon sports. I had the time on my hands, and the new-homeschool-mom energy to sit with him whenever he did any schoolwork. Because he was just in 5$^{th}$ grade, we only did a couple of high quality hours of schoolwork each day overall. It was pretty low-stress, and I loved it.

At this point, having been out of school for over 15 years myself, I could barely remember how to add two fractions. I spent a lot of my own time re-learning all my arithmetic. This began out of a sense of responsibility to Alex, but I very quickly found math to be so much more fun and interesting than I ever had found it to be when I was in school. By re-learning it all myself, with the purpose of teaching him, I was becoming truly enthusiastic about it. I started having my own "Oh, I get it!" moments, which feel great. What I now know is that learning math ideally should be a string of these moments, closely tied together.

Because I had the time and Alex had the interest we just fell into the Full-Contact way of doing math. We didn't do a lot of math, but what we did, we did together. This was very lucky for us, and I am well aware that if Alex had not been as enthusiastic about math, or if I had been busier or more distracted at that time in our lives, everything about our approach to math might have turned out differently.

Scott, Alex's younger brother, is just as smart as Alex, but he's somewhat less *excited* about math. Put it this way, Scott never once asked me for "Bigger multiplication problems, please Mom!" If he had been my first child, I might have done things differently. Luckily for him, however, by the time he too decided to try homeschooling, I was already in the habit of teaching math Full-Contact.

I can honestly say that when the boys were young I never once made them go off and do a worksheet. During those early math years we did it together or we didn't do it at all. This wasn't something I set out to do, it is just what I see that I did, looking back on it now.

## Chapter One: Full-Contact Math

I vividly remembered two things I hated about learning math from my own school years. The first one was having to do hundreds of identical problems in a row. It was boring drudgery! If I knew it well enough to do the first one or two, why do the others? I *was* a pretty chatty kid, so maybe they were just trying to keep me busy!

The other thing I hated was having to sit and wait for help when I was stuck on a problem. It bugged me to get stuck on a simple little question and to have to just sit there, staring into space for five minutes, waiting my turn for the teacher. It's not like reading where you can just gloss over a word you don't know, or quickly look it up and keep reading. In math, if you are stuck on one little thing, the entire problem grinds to a halt.

I guess those memories were formative for me, and I consciously decided never to give the boys rote practice and to always be immediately available for questions.

I was intimately involved in every math thing they did. For years I never gave them a problem I couldn't solve myself. I sat with them while they worked, or at the very worst, I did the dishes while they worked at the kitchen table, ready to sit with them at a moment's notice.

I kept our sessions short and sweet, and we never did math if we were tired or rushed. The boys never did rote practice, and math became an *active-thought* activity for the whole family. Math was something we did together with our brains turned on!

Whatever I was doing seemed to work. The boys were "ahead" and scored really well on standardized tests – but much more importantly, math was an enjoyable and interesting activity that we shared together.

I knew this approach to teaching my kids math was fun as well as productive, but it wasn't until I briefly <u>didn't</u> do it that I learned how important it really was. A couple of years ago my family went through a very stressful and hectic period.

Money was even tighter than usual, and so I took a job working three days a week as a personal assistant for a local woman in her home. Scott was twelve at the time, and he would usually come with me. He'd bring his school work, and would be able to get a few hours done, sitting in her dining room while I worked upstairs. I usually insisted on at least two hours of work each time we were there, and then he was free to do what he wanted, like play outside, or play his video games.

I always gave him a good stack of math problems to do, with the idea that I'd correct them and sit with him later. But since it was such a hectic time in my life, later often didn't come, or I'd correct his problems quickly and hurriedly explain a couple of things to him as I was thinking about the laundry or trying to figure out how to be in three places at one time.

I knew, in the back of my mind, that this was not ideal. But I told myself that he was getting a lot of math done (putting in a lot of time), and even if I really didn't know if he was learning anything, I assumed he probably was figuring it out. I had even started to give him more math problems than usual, partly to keep him busy, partly to assuage my unacknowledged guilt. I should have known better, but it was just too appealing to start using math as a keep-busy activity, and then to feel like math was "getting done," simply because he was spending time on it.

It didn't take long before I saw some changes in Scott's behavior and attitude toward math. He pretty quickly realized that I wouldn't always check his work, so he wouldn't always do it, or at least not all of it. Because he had so many problems to get through, I had unwittingly set him up to try to rush through them so he could go play. This wanting to rush through his problems led him to quitting problems as soon as they were a little tricky or tedious.

## Chapter One: Full-Contact Math

He started skipping or missing questions that I felt he could have done if he'd tried, so of course I started admonishing him to try harder. He started making more silly mistakes, so I started admonishing him to be more diligent. He wasn't trying as hard. He was enjoying math less and less. Our "math conversations" were becoming more critical on my part and more defensive on his.

I knew that the hands-on, Full-Contact approach was the way to go. I had done it for years and found it to be both productive and rewarding. Yet when things in my life got really hectic, I had unthinkingly fallen into the trap of just assigning Scott work and pushing him off. I think I was hoping that it would be good enough and work out somehow.

Luckily, I recognized what was going on. I made a decision to get back on track, and go back to what I knew worked. Scott would only do math if I was physically sitting with him, paying attention, even if it meant he would do less of it! Quickly his attitude was transformed, and his skills started improving again.

Many of us, even those of us who ought to know better, fall into this type of disconnected math teaching, because we are simply too busy. On the other hand, others among us have never even considered teaching math in any other way. We teach math the traditional way, as we ourselves were taught, and we simply don't realize that math can, and should, be taught differently!

It is an iconic image in today's culture: the math student, sweating over his problems, alone in a room. We have no cultural images of families "mathing" together. Families on

TV may discuss politics around the dinner table, but never math. Math has a bad reputation as a boring yet necessary evil, to be gotten through with about as much pleasure as going to the dentist!

In our culture we have a clear notion of how math should be taught: You show them a new concept, and then send them off to practice, practice, practice. Practice makes perfect! Later, you go over what they got wrong. The majority of kids' math time is spent alone, and the time spent with you is stuffy and dry on one end, and critical on the other. We believe that math is mostly learned off on your own, through hours of repetitive practice. This is simply how it is done.

Textbooks perpetuate this myth by suggesting that the "right" book is all you need. They promise to require very little time on your part, even suggesting that with their book your kid can basically teach himself math! Like a magic diet, the "right" textbook will miraculously allow your child to learn math without any involvement on your part. Unfortunately, like most miracle diets, that approach doesn't work.

Sarah, a local homeschool mom, asked me to do a math evaluation of her youngest daughter last year. I had known the family for several years on the homeschool circuit, and I knew her kids as very bright, articulate high achievers who regularly won competitions like Science Olympiad and Odyssey of the Mind. I knew Sarah to be a warm and loving, conscientious mother who put a tremendous amount of time and energy into her kids.

Sarah was concerned because Katherine, her youngest, wasn't scoring well on practice standardized tests, and Sarah didn't really understand why. She thought that Katherine had already covered most of the topics in her

## Chapter One: Full-Contact Math

textbook and that she had actually done quite well on them at the time. But she wasn't really sure. Sarah wasn't sure whether Katherine was forgetting information she had already learned, or if she had never learned the concepts in the first place.

Before I sat down with Katherine, Sarah explained her homeschooling math approach to me: Each day she assigned her kids about an hour's worth of math problems. They did the work up in their rooms during the course of the day, and the next morning Sarah corrected it. They were then supposed to go back on their own and see if they could figure out what they got wrong. She did not go over their mistakes with them herself, but she did have a private tutor for them once a week for any questions they might have.

Having known Katherine for several years as a cheerful, bright kid, I was floored when I sat down to work with her. Every vibe emanating from her body said she didn't want to be there. She was suddenly abrupt and sulky. She so clearly didn't want to be doing this, and I was a bit taken aback by her attitude.

But, I am a professional math tutor, so that attitude is nothing new to me. We got down to work. Her skills were actually pretty good, but it was like pulling teeth. As soon as a problem took more than one or two steps, she balked. During one problem, it was obvious that the next thing to do was a big, ugly long division. She just stopped and stared blankly, as if she had no idea what to do. However, by this point in my evaluating her, I knew without a doubt that she absolutely *did* know what to do! She just didn't *want* to do it. She may have hoped I'd just give her the answer, or do it for her, or just move on.

I have seen this attitude countless times with kids. They simply do not *want* to turn on their brains and actively use that muscle to solve a problem. They haven't made that decision to *try*. In fact they have made a, possibly unconscious, decision *not* to try, and to *only* do that which comes easily and immediately. You can almost *see* them realizing that the next step in a problem will take a little work, and then trying to avoid it. It is a common form of math rebellion, a tactic used by many, many kids who hate math: "You can make me sit here, but you can't make me try."

So it was with Katherine, and trust me, that hour was as bad for me as it was for her. She was much, much more capable than she was presenting. Her mother told me that it was always like this. In fact, she said, it was like this all the time with both of her kids.

Katherine's stumbling block with math was psychological, not technical. She simply hated math: The process of it, the idea of it, the book, the pencil. Ugh! Everything about it was awful! Every problem she solved was done under duress, almost against her own will. Math was "pointless and boring." In Katherine's mind, math had come to represent lots of yelling, forced solitary, and drudgery.

Being a "good kid," however, she wasn't going to rebel overtly, but she certainly wasn't going to put her brain into it. They say that you can lead a horse to water but you can't make it drink, right? Well you can lead a kid to her math book, but you can't make her think!

The diagnosis I gave her mother was this: Katherine's math skills are just fine. Her trouble with math is emotional. Until you fix that, anything you do is a waste of time.

This was an "Aha!" moment for Sarah. It rang true and made sense to her. This, the *emotional* component, was what was broken in their approach to math! The *attitude*,

## Chapter One: Full-Contact Math

not the skills, had to be fixed! She had been at her wits' end for a long time, trying to figure out why her kids weren't progressing well in math, when they were so obviously bright. Now she knew!

Sarah had thought she was doing everything right: she used the right curriculum, she made the kids work at their exercises every day, – she even had a math tutor for them! However, what Sarah hadn't told me earlier about her idyllic-sounding approach to teaching math was that it involved threats, punishments and daily battles over procrastination and sloppy work. She was basically force-feeding them. What she didn't realize is that as long as kids "hate" math, anything we force feed them will get spit right out!

Sarah's traditional approach to teaching math had seemed to be fine when the kids were quite young: Jonathan, the oldest, tested in the 94th percentile when he was 10. But over time, she said, his comparative performance and attitude toward math had gone downhill, while his other studies were still going well. Katherine's story was pretty similar: an obviously bright kid, starting out well and above average, who then gradually started slipping behind while becoming more and more negative.

Sarah had reacted to her children's resistance in the typical way: she grew stricter and sterner. She *knew* they were bright kids, so she chalked their math negativity up to kids being kids, and didn't think much of it because "doesn't everyone hate math?" She sent them off to do more exercises, exhorting them to try harder and stay focused. This made them dislike math more. Then started the internal rebellions, the silly mistakes, the procrastinating, the lack of any initiative in problem-solving. Naturally, this made Sara more strict in turn. And so on. Years of this downward spiral, despite Sarah *truly* having the best intentions all along the way, had made both of her kids hate math.

Even though the situation was getting worse and worse, Sarah diligently kept at it, afraid after a certain point that if she *didn't* force them they'd surely never learn anything! And by the time I worked with her family, this was probably true. Sarah felt stuck and trapped. Her kids were unhappy with the situation and so was she. They were really smart kids. She knew this, but they could not, or would not, do well at math, and she could not figure out why. By the time she met me, she was considering sending them both back to school.

Over years, for many families, math slowly becomes associated with isolation and criticism. "Math time" with the parent is us either lecturing them, or critiquing their mistakes. Math is not something we share and enjoy together. It has very few precious memories associated with it, but many, many negative ones. Despite our best intentions, we are training them to hate math!

Almost every kid I know who hates math has been taught in the typical disconnected way so common in our culture today, even among homeschoolers. Sarah and her husband were well-educated, well-intentioned parents who devoted all their time and resources to their children, yet they turned out three more American kids who hate math, and who, unfortunately, have lots of company.

## Break the Cycle of Math Abuse!

Sometimes parents are too busy to sit down to math with their kids on a regular basis. Sometimes they simply don't consider a better way. But sometimes, however, parents won't spend "math time" with their kids because they have their own, long-standing negative feelings about math.

Psychologists say that people who are abused start to believe the things that are said about them, no matter how untrue they may be. Many adults spend years trying to replace negative mental thoughts with positive ones, usually with the help of a therapist, at significant cost of time and money.

Not to diminish the seriousness of real abuse, which is truly a terrible problem, but I think that some of the same principles are at work in many of us! In some sense, many of us are victims of <u>math abuse</u>!

Many of us homeschool parents went to school ourselves. Some of us had negative experiences. We were taught poorly, by poor teachers and then told we were bad at math. Really, it was their fault, not ours. We were victims of poor, boring, inadequate teaching, but then we were told it was us – that *we* were stupid, inadequate, uninterested! Not knowing any better, nor having any frame of reference, we believed these messages. These feelings of dislike and inadequacy became internalized and have gone unhealed and unchallenged. Until now.

I fervently believe that there is no such thing as being "bad at math." There is only inadequate teaching. *Anyone* can easily learn basic mathematics if it presented in a clear, consistent, step-by-step way in a stress-free, supportive environment.

A childhood of negative math memories naturally makes us shy away from spending math time with our kids. Why would we want to do anything that brings up those negative feelings? Conscious or unconscious negative feelings about math show up in both our actions and comments, and frequently get passed on to our kids.

Even if we weren't told that we were bad at math, the tedium of our math classes throughout the years is a strong enough negative memory to make us avoid math time now. We have internalized without question the fact that math has to be painfully boring.

The trouble is, we just perpetuate the cycle. We don't want to sit down with that book and try to remember how to add two fractions, because it just brings up all those negative feelings. Then, when our child starts becoming disinterested or overwhelmed, we say "Well, he's just bad at math like me."

Many of us choose to homeschool because our own school experience was dry, dull, ineffective and definitely not inspirational! We now believe that there is a better way, and we are determined to provide it for our children. We truly believe that learning can and *should* be fascinating.

We hear other homeschool parents declare all the time that they used to *hate* history in high school, but that now they love it. They are teaching history to their kids in exciting, interesting ways, quite unlike the dry lectures they got in school. They love history, their kids love history, it's all good!

Why does that turnaround happen for history so frequently, yet a math-hater always stays a math-hater? It's a given that many of us had at least one or two terrible math teachers in our time. This can be a real turn-off. Worse, with a poor math teacher for a year, we can develop gaps in our knowledge, which cause us to struggle even more, further down the road. However, many of us also had some horrible English or history teachers too, yet we can end up

## Chapter One: Full-Contact Math

loving history. Why are we able to break the cycle with those subjects and turn around and teach them to our kids in a brand-new, exciting way?

Many of us graduate from school thinking that math, history and literature are *all* boring, dry and useless subjects. We got very little inspiration from any of our teachers, and the information they provided seemed completely irrelevant to us. We knew the names and dates but not the connections. We knew the plot, setting and characters, but not the human motivations. We went through the motions of solving equations without really knowing or caring why it worked. We memorized, took the test, and promptly forgot everything over and over.

Healing our attitude toward history and literature frequently happens accidentally. At some point after we graduated from school, maybe we accidentally stumbled across a fascinating historical documentary, perhaps by channel surfing on a lazy Sunday afternoon. Or we were bored on vacation and the only book around was a History of Something, and we found that we couldn't put it down. We accidentally figure out on our own that history can be endlessly fascinating, if presented well. For most of us, this was a revelation. History didn't have to be as dull as our teachers had made it – it was *them*, not us! Most of us now teach history to our kids, <u>not</u> the way it was taught to us in school, but in the way we discovered that we loved it ourselves. We are excited by it, and pass that enthusiasm on to our kids.

Even if we never pick up Shakespeare again after high school, most of us have since then read books we simply couldn't put down. Because we can pick and choose what to read now, and we discover something we *enjoy* reading, we read more frequently and more enthusiastically. So even if we hated English in high school, very few of us claim we hate reading, or are not good at it. Even people who would never read a novel with more than a 5th grade vocabulary, (which is actually most of the Adult Bestseller list) don't consider themselves "bad" at reading, or have a negative attitude toward it.

But there is very little opportunity for this kind of healing from our math schooling. "Math talk" simply is not a part of our culture. We are unlikely to accidentally turn on a math lecture and find it riveting – first of all because there just aren't too many on TV, and secondly because the chances of the topic being at exactly the right level for us is remote. The topic would have to be easy enough for us to understand, yet challenging enough to be interesting. We are also unlikely to accidentally pick up a math book and find that we love it, for exactly the same reasons.

So our negative opinion of math never gets healed. We never discover a different way to learn it. We never discover how rich and fun and fascinating it really can be! In fact, as we grow up, math becomes associated with even *more* negative things, like taxes, mortgages and health care!

If we have never had one joyous, positive or enjoyable math experience, is it any wonder that we consciously or unconsciously shy away from "math time" with our kids?

Many psychologists say that the first step to healing is admitting we have a problem. If you have negative feelings about math, that's not necessarily a big deal. If it is affecting your children, that *is* a big deal. Our kids really do need to master at least basic math skills for practical reasons, if not advanced math skills to go on to higher education.

## Chapter One: Full-Contact Math

"Math time" together is probably the most important thing you can do for your kids to help them succeed in math. I cannot emphasize enough how critical this is. You can get the most raved-about Asian math book, but unless you start to spend math time together, doing problems together, talking about them together, bonding over these things and generating an association of warmth and love with math, in addition to developing skills, you will be pushing a rock uphill.

There are many great video courses and short videos that you can watch together. But stay focused and be there. Don't plop your kid in front of the TV and wander off. That tells him that you consider math unimportant. At least less important than the laundry! Plop in a video, grab a blanket, some hot chocolate and the remote, and hunker down, *together*. Pause the video a lot. Comment on it. Be interested in it.

*Sit* with your kid while he does his math problems – each and every one of them. See what you are putting him through! Don't let it be a lonely experience. If he gets stuck, be there to help him. Be engaged. Nothing feels better than having mom or dad pay complete, full attention to us!

Five or ten minutes spent with you, with your full attention, will be more productive than an hour of exercises done off in a room by himself.

Bring up a well-solved math problem to Dad when he comes home. Even if it was just $2 + 2 = 4$! Why is a math accomplishment worth *less* praise than that brown and green splotch that your daughter proudly proclaimed to be a tree, which you hung so proudly on your refrigerator? Why is a well-solved long-division problem *less* impressive than that squeaky violin piece you made the whole family sit and listen to? We celebrate their efforts in other areas all the time; why not applaud their efforts in math with the same enthusiasm we show for everything else?

You will find that as you do your math together, it will become part of your daily conversation. It will become something you talk about, even when you are not specifically working on math. You will have funny moments, as well as frustrating ones. You will share little victories, as well as little failures. A family math history will develop. It will be something your family has built together, which will fuel future conversations and jokes. It will be a shared bond.

CHAPTER TWO
# ARITHMETIC AND PRE-ALGEBRA

If your child is still working on arithmetic, or any topic up to and including pre-algebra you are definitely in luck. This is a great time for you to jump in and get started with "Full-Contact" math, *even if you haven't done long division in 20 years*!

The first thing you have to do is brush up on your math skills yourself. Wait! No! Don't shut this book! I promise you, if you are a functioning adult, you can absolutely do this. There is absolutely no reason, other than time and desire, that you cannot re-learn these math skills. At this stage in his math development, your child is *not* so far ahead that you can't quickly catch up. Most of it will come back to you pretty easily. Maybe some topics will need a little more thought, and you might have to try a couple of different books or videos to figure them out. But I promise you that you *can* figure any of it out, if you want to. I know it sounds like a lot of (boring) work, but trust me, it is money in the bank. If you get really involved now, it will save you countless hours in the future. It will save you hours of nagging, cajoling and punishing, and it will save your child countless hours of frustration and confusion. It will save you many hours and dollars spent trying to find just the "right" curriculum. It will also save you many hours of doubt and anguish as you watch your kid struggle and fall behind.

You may think that "those people" who actually sit and do math with their kids just remember everything they ever learned about math from school. That is most definitely not true! We *all* forget techniques we never use. The fact that you can't remember exactly how to do long division is not surprising. What will be surprising is how quickly it will all come back to you. Math is two things: it is a bunch of ideas and a bunch of techniques. People tend to remember ideas, but forget techniques. We all understand the idea of division, even if we forget the technique of long division. We understand the idea of multiplication, even if we forget the technique for 5-digit, decimal-number multiplication. And after years of negotiating "sharing" with our kids, we all understand the idea of adding fractions! However, most of us forget the *technique* used to do this.

Without revisiting these techniques periodically, everyone forgets them. I was a math major during my first year in college, but when I started to homeschool Alex and Scott, I couldn't remember how to add two fractions! I had to sit down and re-learn everything all over again.

Math really has to be learned sequentially. One concept leads to the next and so on. Your child can't skip a concept, or he will get lost somewhere down the line. As a homeschool parent you should brush up on the skills leading up to whatever math topic your child is currently working on. For example, if he is on long division, all you need to know is how to add, subtract and multiply. If he's already onto simple equations, there is a bit more for you to review.

It is not as hard as you might think. You really *can* do it. It won't take as much time as you are afraid it will, and not only will it benefit your child tremendously, it will also

## Chapter Two: Arithmetic and Pre-Algebra

enrich your own life. If it takes you a week, a month or even six months, it will be so worth it!

Until you really understand your child's math problems, how will you know *why* he is getting them wrong? How will you know if he is just making silly mistakes or if he is actually having trouble with comprehension? Silly mistakes are pretty unimportant at a very young age, but comprehension problems need to be addressed so that he can move forward. As his parent, you absolutely *have* to know which of these things is happening. Then, and only then, will you be able to know if your child has mastered the ideas and techniques he needs to go forward.

Many of us homeschool parents use textbooks with answer keys, and we actually give our kid grades. Grades are supposed to give us an idea of how well our student understands the material, but they can sometimes be misleading. A child might get 50% of a set of problems wrong, yet totally understand the idea and the technique. Perhaps he's just young, excited and rushing. Sometimes the brain goes faster than the hand and things get jumbled, but he "gets it" completely. What he really needs is just to get a little older, a little more mature and slow down a bit.

On the other hand, your child might be getting almost all of the problems right, and still not really "get it." Many of us might feel okay if our kid was getting 80% of her math problems correct. And that really might be okay. An 80% in some textbooks is pretty impressive. Maybe she understands everything perfectly, and just made silly mistakes on 20% of the problems. But on the other hand, *maybe she only understands 80% of the concepts she needs to know to move on*! That could lead to disaster.

Unless you understand the ideas and know how to do the techniques yourself, you will not really know if your child is ready to move forward. There is just no way to avoid it: You need to sit down with the books and do some review. You might even enjoy it! Ideally you would start at the beginning and brush up on each topic, <u>on your own</u>, until you got to the same point as your child. Then you can easily sit with her and help her with all of her problems. Once you have done this, it is relatively easy for you to stay one step ahead of her, all the way.

One good way for you to brush up is to watch videos. There are a number of excellent video series that teach math in a really nice, clear way. You could get yourself one that starts with the very beginning topics. You and your child can watch it together. It will be good for both of you. If you need to watch one segment three times, then maybe she does too! Caution: you will still need to go off and make sure that you can really *do* the exercises. It is one thing to watch a video and follow along. It is something else entirely to sit down and actively do the problems.

If you really can't take the time to catch up before you start sitting and helping her with her math, then try this: first brush up on whatever she is currently working on, then go back and review the ideas that led up to that point. If you do this, however, please first read the section in this chapter entitled "Above All, do no Harm."

After brushing up on your own skills, the next thing you need to do is to take your math Full-Contact. To do this all you have to do is make a decision, and then stick to it. You have to decide that <u>any and all math that your child does, will be done with you at his side</u>. I cannot emphasize enough the importance of this!

❈ ❈ ❈

## Chapter Two: Arithmetic and Pre-Algebra

When our kids are very young we read counting and number books to them all the time. We teach them their numbers with enthusiasm and delight. They are so smart!

Soon, as interested, concerned parents, we discover in the stores all the math workbooks for young children. Each page may have 20 addition problems on them, made *super-fun* by the picture of the teddy bear holding balloons! These are skills-practice books, created by professionals who obviously know a lot more about this than we do.

When we buy the book for little Jenny, she is very excited, and when we get home, she may sit and happily do her workbook exercises. Books have always been fun for her, and now she feels smart, like a big girl! For us, this is great. Not only is she happily occupied and not under our heels for 10 minutes, but she is also doing something productive. We have found something to occupy her time for a few minutes that doesn't come with the guilt of TV or videogames!

And I guess this would be fine if we stopped there, and she stayed happy. If only we *kept* it to five or ten minutes at a pop. But we don't. It is too tempting. If she happily does ten minutes then we give her more next time. We tell her to sit down at her workbook more frequently. We start to use it as a "time to get things done." We keep increasing the amount we give her to do, until she starts to complain. Until then, math is just a gift of free time for us, which is golden! Then, one day she doesn't want to do her math book at all, and we get miffed. We had *counted* on that few minutes of precious time – to make a phone call or do the dishes. Because it is "productive" we *make* her do it. Ostensibly this is for her own good, but really it is just so that we can go fold the laundry. Math becomes a way for us to get a few minutes of free time without the guilt. In fact, we feel pretty good about it!

That's why those workbooks, even for first-graders, are so popular. Teachers and parents alike desperately need a few undisturbed minutes, and that is who those books cater to. They are selling the idea that your kids can learn math while you go do something else, like give another child face-to-face attention, or breastfeed your baby! However, it doesn't work in school, and it doesn't work at home.

When we use math as make-busy work, little Jenny will inevitably start to complain or lose interest. Math has become an *alone* activity, and it no longer makes her feel smart and special. She doesn't want to do math alone – she wants to do it with her *mom*!

The Full-Contact approach would have mom always sit with Jenny, fully involved, while she worked in her book. They would do it only as long as Jenny was fully engaged, and then they would stop. Jenny would keep on feeling special, and she would enjoy her workbook more and more. Mom would not be trying to do three other things at the same time and be only half-listening. She would be fully present, enthusiastically involved, even if it is only for five minutes.

This Full-Contact approach is beneficial in two major ways. First, we parents are there to help our kids as soon as they get stuck, which reduces frustration and makes their math time much more productive. Second, we are associating math time with our loving attention, which is extremely powerful.

Reading experts also tell us that when a child is just starting to read we shouldn't push him to figure out each and every word he doesn't know phonetically. It is okay, they say, to make him sound words out occasionally, but in general the best thing to do is simply tell him what the word is. This is because simply telling him the word is still helpful and instructive, and they don't want us turning storytime into drudgery!

Use the same idea to guide you in knowing exactly how much help to give your kid on his math. You want to help him when he gets stuck so that he can quickly and happily move forward. On the other hand, you don't want to do it all for him!

The tough news is that you *are* going to sit with your kid while he works through each and every math problem you want him to do. The *good* news, however, is that you actually won't have to spend that much time doing it!

I hate to give absolute numbers for how long your sit-down sessions should be, because kids are all different. Keep working as long as your child is interested and engaged. Aim to stop *before* he loses focus. I can tell you that I rarely did math for more than 15 minutes at a time with Alex or Scott before the age of 12. More importantly at this stage, is for you to do math with your kid each and every day. Maybe twice. But keep each session brief. You must stop before his eyes glaze over.

People are generally surprised that I recommend only about 15 to 30 minutes daily a day of sit-down, face-to-face math problem time at this stage. For many families this is much less than their child has been doing, and they are skeptical.

The flip side of my recommendation is, however, that it has to be done daily. 15 minutes a day is a *hundred* times better than one three-hour session each week!

Many families will find it a challenge to do this consistently. It takes a real commitment. Many doctors say that we should get half an hour of exercise each day. We all know how hard that can be! It takes a certain level of commitment and dedication to exercise daily. I would love to do this myself, but the days just get away from me somehow, and before I know it a week has passed. I would love to be able to exercise for four hours in one shot and get the same benefits – but I think I'd end up in the hospital! You can only exercise so much at one time, and you can't do it in irregular bursts. Ask any "weekend warrior!" The way to get and stay in shape is daily exercise. So, too with math.

If we don't make time for our kid to do her math consistently and then one day suddenly realize that two weeks have gone by and she hasn't done any, what do we do? Freak out, usually! We might make her feel bad that she hasn't done any math, even though it's completely unrealistic to imagine that she would just go do it on her own. Often at this point, we do a marathon session or two. We panic because she has forgotten techniques, and then she feels even worse. It's not a pleasant experience for anyone. We declare a new rule, such as, "Do 15 minutes every day before you brush your teeth," and then leave it up to her to do it.

Kids are notoriously bad at time management, even when they are super-motivated, so this is just unreasonable. Very few kids at the arithmetic or pre-algebra stage are mature, responsible and enthusiastic enough to manage their own math work schedule. Maybe we *are* trying to teach time-management, but at what expense? If we were really serious about them doing some math every day, we wouldn't leave the responsibility completely up to them.

But this is all beside the point. Now that we know how important it is to take it Full-Contact, we're going to be sitting down to her work with her each time. It is now going to have to fit in with our schedule, so making the time for it is going to be up to *us*. Now she won't need to have good time-management skills *before* she learns how to subtract a negative number!

As parents, we need to provide the space and time to sit and do math with our kids each and every day. You need to be there to give her your attention. You need to be in a quiet space. And preferably not when friends and family are off at the circus or out for ice cream. That will *really* make her hate math! It needs to be a quiet, stress-free, nice time for the two of you.

I say to try to do this every day, because stuff always comes up. Life gets in the way; if you aim for every day, you'll probably get in 5 days a week, which is fine. But if you *aim* for five days a week, you might only get in two or three, which is not really enough. You will then be tempted to do extra math on one day to make up for it, which is not nearly as effective.

## Practice makes Zombies!

Many arithmetic and pre-algebra books have pages and pages of virtually identical problems. Rote practice like this often shuts down kids brains. By the time they get to the tenth problem, they are just going through the motions. By assigning work like this and sending them off to do it, we are actually *preventing* learning from occurring! We set our kids up to do math on automatic. This is a real concern, because over time many kids start to expect *all* math to be done that way. Anything that doesn't come automatically without thinking just can't be done. They think math is supposed to be done in that zombie-like, unthinking way! Rote practice turns off the brain and should be avoided at all costs.

The Full-Contact math approach fixes this problem. If you really want your kid to do a full page of multiplication problems, then I urge you to sit with him for the entire time. See what you are putting him through. If it is too boring for you, it is *way* too boring for him!

## If only I could just find the *Perfect* Curricula!

Many of us homeschool parents are way too fixated on finding the perfect curriculum. We think that if we get just the right curriculum for our kids' learning style, some kind of magic will happen. I have definitely been guilty of this one myself!

The reality is that most textbooks are just fine. *Which* one you use is so much less important than *how* you use it. Just like the "right" type of exercise is the one that you enjoy, the "right" textbook is one that you like!

A textbook is a bit of a safety net for a homeschool parent. We feel that if we use one we won't miss any important topics, all bases will be covered. And that, generally, is true.

However, I have never met a textbook that wasn't lacking *something* for each of my kids; that didn't put a topic that I thought was too hard too soon, or too easy too late. No one textbook is going to be just what your kid needs all the time. On some topics there may be way too much repetition and your kid is bored to tears. Other topics may get breezed over, because they were covered in the previous book, which unfortunately he did not have. If you don't like the way your textbook explains something, try a different book or video lecture. There are tons of great resources out there these days.

Be aware, too, that many textbooks are used to teach kids who have a very wide range of skills. It may not be expected, or even appropriate for your kid to do *all* the exercises at the end of the chapter. The problems in a textbook often range from simple and basic to extremely difficult, so teachers can use them for a wide range of classes. Schools pick and choose what exercises from a textbook to assign, and even which topics to skip. So should you.

Also, in my opinion, most textbooks have way *too many* exercises, and if you insist that your child do them all, you will burn him out and dull his enthusiasm. Remember the rule: Sit with him when he works, and stop working before his eyes glaze over.

I never used a "curriculum" per se, at this stage for either of my boys. I used lots of them! When Alex started homeschooling I was lucky enough to read one of those books "What Your $5^{th}$ Grader Needs to Know." For me, it was a great tool. It simply listed the math concepts he needed to master at that stage, and gave a very brief explanation of them. I used that book as my guide to *which* skills he needed to have. I used other books and videos to help me learn them. I did not do a whole $5^{th}$ grade curriculum, which I think both of my boys would have found pretty tedious. We quickly moved on to the $6^{th}$ grade list of topics, and I was quite disappointed that the series didn't go any further. I was now on my own figuring out the next step.

Whenever we were working on a topic, be it "positives and negatives," or "percentages," I would study the topic on my own, using various different books. Then when I understood it myself, I'd teach it to them. This approach worked for me for several reasons. First, it got me *completely* involved. I wasn't relying on any book to teach them. I was relying on the book to teach *me*. Second, I get bored easily, so this allowed me to switch things up a bit, use different books and videos without creating absolute chaos for my kids. Sometimes I'd have them watch videos with me, sometimes I'd even read to them from a math book, but for the most part I just taught myself from the books and then taught it to them.

Please don't feel that *you* have to do it this way. It worked for me, but any good curriculum that you understand will work just fine. The topics will already be in order for you, and the explanations right there. Just remember that you can always supplement with other books and videos if need be, and that you don't have to do all the problems in any given section.

If you are using a curriculum, and your child is struggling, don't be too quick to rush to judgment on the textbook. When a kid starts to struggle, it is often not that the new topics are unclearly written, it is usually that the *old* stuff from last year wasn't mastered well enough! Often a student seems to be going along fine and then one year starts to struggle. We blame the new textbook, so we get a different one. That one's apparently no good either, so we keep looking. Without really knowing exactly *what* her stumbling blocks are, because we have forgotten our own math, we will not be able to figure out if the problem really *is* the textbook. Maybe she is simply not prepared, and does not have the skills to be doing what we have put in front of her.

If you find yourself in this situation, I suggest you go back to the beginning. Using the checklist in the back of the book, check to see that she understands all the ideas, and can do all the techniques that lead up to where you think she should be. I know it seems like a drag, and you may be panicking because you are already "behind," but these early math skills are absolutely vital to continued math success. You don't have to re-do the whole curriculum. Just check that your child understands all the pre-requisite topics. If she can't do arithmetic, she will never get through algebra!

## Above all, do no harm!

Never, ever sit down to help your child with a math problem that you are not totally confident that you can solve! What this means is, unless you are 100% confident of your skills, you should have previously worked through each and every problem you give him to do.

What! Am I really saying that you should do the problems yourself before your child does? That is *exactly* what I am saying. There is nothing worse for a kid who is struggling, than to have you, his parent, sit down and fumble your way through the problem – thinking out loud, having a couple of false starts, making a couple of mistakes and then *finally* figuring it out. By the time you *do* figure it out, your child is completely confused. And what if you *can't* figure it out? I have found that many, many parents really confuse their kids with the on-the-spot "help" they give them. Your kid will get frustrated because you really are being no help at all. You are, in fact, often making it worse. You, then, get frustrated because he is being ungrateful and you really are *just* trying to help! Each time you do this you lose credibility in his eyes. How is he going to know *when* to listen to you? If you are always saying, "Forget what I said 5 minutes ago, this is how you really do it," he will begin to doubt you. It is also very stressful for him, and a waste of time, so don't do it.

Unless you absolutely understand the topic inside and out, and you are *sure* that you can figure out – *on the spot* – anything he throws at you, do him a favor. Go off by yourself and figure it out. Think about how to explain it, then come back to him and do so.

Until your child is ready to go off and do his problems on his own – and yes, the time will come – I suggest that you absolutely make sure you can do and explain every single problem you sit down to do with him. If you can't figure it out, maybe it is a good one to skip.

Since you will now no longer be assigning him a gazillion problems to do, this preparation will actually *not* take you a tremendous amount of time. Remember to sit right with him, fully engaged, the whole time he works through his problems. Keep your sessions short. Keep math an alert, focused, together activity.

If you absolutely *must* give him problems to do while you are occupied elsewhere, and you don't have time to work through the problems yourself beforehand, then you can do this: Tell him to skip any problem he does not understand easily. Then, later, when you *do* have time, go over the problems he skipped or got wrong *by yourself* and figure them out. Then when you are sure that you know how to do each one he missed, sit and go over them with him. If, at this point, you still can't figure it out, simply tell him that, and maybe you can come back to it another time. Maybe the answer key has a typo, or maybe it is just an unusually hard problem.

I know that this does sound like a lot of work. However, this preparedness on your part will reduce frustration for both you and your child. Learning math is a much more *emotional* process than you might think. If there is tension, fear or confusion, I don't care how *long* you work, nothing is going to get mastered. Stress, chaos and rushing are enemies of math learning! You need to create a calm, quiet space and time for you and your child to peacefully and productively do math together.

The more time and energy you put into this when your kids are younger, the easier it will be when they are older and the less time overall you will have to spend. The hours you spend now, brushing up on your own long-forgotten math skills and sitting with your child while he solves arithmetic problems, will be hours you won't spend years from now battling over math!

## Calculators

I have mixed feelings about the use of calculators at this stage in the game. It is very important for kids to develop "number sense." Doing math without calculators really does help with this. As our kids go forward, math life really is easier if they just *know* that 3 x 8 = 24.

Ideally, they would all be able to spit out all their multiplication facts automatically. However, in reality, they usually have a few they can't always remember immediately without pause, like 8 x 7. I still forget what that is myself! And even if you know your times table, arithmetic like three-digit multiplication or long-division is always pretty tedious.

Many kids, boys especially for some reason that I don't understand, also seem to *hate* writing at this stage. From all their moaning and complaining, you might think that writing is physically painful for them! So while they *can* do triple-digit multiplication, it is a slow, agonizing process that just takes all the fun out of a potentially interesting problem.

When I was first teaching Alex how to solve simple equations, I let him use a calculator for all the multiplication and division. I wanted him to focus on the *new* idea he was learning – the idea that both sides of an equation must always stay in balance. He was a slow and laborious writer, and while he could do the arithmetic, it was pretty tedious for him. He was enthusiastic about math, and I wanted to keep it that way. No matter how "good" you may be at three-digit multiplication, it is still pretty slow and boring!

Math is easiest to learn <u>one</u> new idea at a time. Each new idea should follow easily from the understanding of previous ideas. If those previous ideas are a struggle, it will make the new idea really hard to learn.

Think about the skill needed to add two fractions. This is possibly one of the most frequently forgotten math techniques of all time. First of all, you need to understand the *idea* of adding fractions. But you also have to be able to add and multiply numbers as well. If those two things are still a challenge, or even just laboriously slow, then adding fractions is going to be a seriously unpleasant experience. In fact, it is very likely that the big idea of the technique, the Common Denominator, will get lost in the struggle over arithmetic.

If your child is still struggling with basic arithmetic, you have two choices. You could work with him until his adding, subtracting, multiplication and division skills are flawless and answers come easily. Or you could allow him to use a calculator for the adding and multiplication. This way

## Chapter Two: Arithmetic and Pre-Algebra

he can focus on the whole procedure of adding two fractions, while not getting burned out by the arithmetic. My kids were ready, willing and able to go on to bigger and better ideas way before arithmetic became quick and easy for them, so I let them use a calculator. However, that really might not be the right choice for you.

If you want to have them master their arithmetic before moving on, then just realize that there is a limit to how "good" at it they are going to get. I have seen parents assign pages of long-division to their kid, day after day, and then be amazed that they are *still* getting so many wrong! Personally, I think it is a bit of a set-up. Unless your kid has a borderline obsessive-compulsive personality, of *course* he's going to get some wrong! First of all, it is just not that interesting. When something is uninteresting it is hard to stay focused on it. When you can't stay focused, you make silly mistakes. Every single long division problem has tons of opportunities for silly mistakes, which then cause the final answer to come out wrong. Before going on to more advanced topics, you *do* need to see if your kid can do long division – but *not* if he can do 20 long-divisions in a row without pause or mistakes!

Allowing kids to occasionally use a calculator frees their brains to concentrate on the other aspects of a problem. But, on the other hand, arithmetic is a skill that we lose without use. Several years ago I signed Alex and Scott up for the AMC 8, a well-known middle school math competition that is really just a written test. When we walked into the testing center, we discovered that this was the first year that calculators were not allowed. We had had no idea! The boys and I quickly chatted about what they'd need to do now by hand, and Alex said, "Wait, how do you do long division again?" It had been quite a while since he'd done it. Scott wasn't rusty at it, but Alex, the *older* one was! So, I quickly showed him how to do it again, and he said, "Oh, yeah, that's right." It was all just fine. I wasn't upset – it made perfect sense to me. It is to be *expected* that they will get rusty on any skill they don't use.

The calculator choice is yours. Be aware that if you *do* allow her to use the calculator all the time, she may get rusty on some techniques. You will then have to revisit them. However, if you *never* allow her to use a calculator, then many of her problems, which are now finally getting interesting, might be more tedious and boring. She may be more absorbed with the details of the multiplication than the overall problem. Both approaches have pros and cons. Now that you know what they are, pick the approach that is right for you and your child.

The Full-Contact approach really is the very best way to teach your child Arithmetic and Pre-Algebra. He will naturally enjoy math, since it means spending time with you, and getting your undivided attention. You are the best teacher for him at this stage, without a doubt. No-one knows him like you do, and no-one is in a better position to see what he gets, what he doesn't, and *why*. You will be able to sit down to math when you are both alert and calm, and put it off when you are not. Because he won't be doing excessive rote practice, math will be a fully engaged, brain-turned-on activity.

CHAPTER THREE
## COMMON PITFALLS

When a kid is struggling or "behind" in math, it is almost never the case that he is just "bad" at math. Unless a child has a learning disability, the cause of the problem is almost always something in the family's approach to teaching math.

While some families are too rigid in their approach to teaching math to their kids, other families are actually too haphazard. If the math approach is too rigid, the kids often end up hating math, like Katherine in the previous chapter. But if the approach is too haphazard, the kids might not hate math, but they won't *know* it! Not only will the kids lack important skills, over time many of them begin to feel inadequate.

Some parents just never "get around" to teaching their kids good, basic math skills. They mean to, but it just never fits in somehow. Other parents are waiting for their kid to show some interest and initiative before they get started.

Studies show that the vocabulary and education level of parents is the number one predictor of a kid's success in language arts. Kids use vocabulary that their parents use, without ever studying it as part of a lesson plan. Kids whose parents are politically aware usually become politically aware themselves without ever sitting down to a lecture.

A lot of language skill and cultural knowledge is passed on as if by osmosis, without any conscious effort on the parents' part.

However, unless, you happen to be sitting around adding fractions all day for fun, and then discussing them with your husband when he comes home from work, Johnny simply is never going to learn math without a conscious, directed effort on your part – it will never happen.

I have seen parents declare their children to be "bad at math" when in reality it is the family's own somewhat haphazard approach to teaching math that is the problem. My friend Laura is wonderfully creative and smart, and her children are truly incredible. Math just has never been high on her list of priorities. Because she herself is so smart, she figures it will all work out. Her family is so busy doing fun, interesting, educational, and important activities that math just doesn't happen very often. Actually, almost never. However, she does realize that her children need to know it, so she will periodically whip out the math books, declare a structure for work-time and get them to work. They will diligently follow the schedule for at *least* two days, but then, life goes on. Things happen, and the math once again falls by the wayside and the schedule is forgotten. Kind of like me every time I start a new diet!

Last summer, during one of her "We need to study math!" extravaganzas, she assigned Susan, her eldest, a page of problems from her workbook. When Susan couldn't remember how to do long division, Laura hit the roof!

## Chapter Three: Common Pitfalls

On Laura's behalf, I will say that the responsibility of parenting itself, let alone the responsibility of homeschooling, can be incredibly agonizing. Compared to school-parents, we have so many more balls to keep up in the air! There is no passing off the burden of responsibility to someone else, like a teacher, and, honestly, who among us has *never* blown a fuse?

When Susan said that she couldn't remember long division it struck a chord of fear in Laura's heart. Susan was 11 years old already, and had been shown this several times! Several things were said that day that were fairly unproductive. The most telling one was: "But I taught you that last year! Why can't you remember it! Come on, I can't keep teaching you the same thing over and over, we'll never get anywhere!" This was followed by a lengthy lecture on the importance of math, and why the kids needed to take it seriously.

Susan was admonished for not understanding how important math is, in spite of the fact that her mother rarely made it a priority herself. But, to me, the worst thing about this exchange was that it was Blaming the Victim. Of *course* Susan couldn't remember long division. It's a technique! She was shown it a couple of times the year before, and then never saw it or used it again. It's not a particularly captivating process in the first place, so it's hardly surprising that two or three exposures to it didn't stay with her for life!

I honestly don't know anyone who is more loving, kind and warm to her children than Laura. Her comment was blurted out in a moment of frustration – frustration caused by Laura's own haphazard approach to teaching math. Laura's "free" approach to teaching worked well with other subjects, so she just assumed it would work with math.

When I commented that it didn't seem surprising at all to me that Susan couldn't remember how to do long division, given that she hadn't done it for a year, and only a few times before that, Laura was taken aback.  She had *never* forgotten long division, so why was her daughter forgetting it? Susan must be bad at math! What Laura was forgetting was that, for better or worse, she had gone to *school*, and been forced to practice her techniques regularly.  As a math tutor and homeschool mom, I can think of lots of things about the typical school approach to teaching math that I don't like, but <u>regular exposure to important techniques</u> is not one of them!

By not wanting to submit her own children to the daily drudgery that she herself had experienced, Laura had gone way too far in the opposite direction.  No, her kids didn't have to suffer boring daily lectures, or go off in isolation for an hour a day to grind out problem after problem, but they weren't getting consistent, regular exposure to math either, which is absolutely vital to progress.

We can't throw the baby out with the bathwater.  Whatever we hated about our school years' math experience, we can't reject absolutely everything about it.

## The Engineer Dad

A quite different problem sometimes arises when one parent is a "math expert."  A surprisingly large number of kids I know who struggle the most with math actually have dads who are engineers.  At first I thought the cases I was seeing were just exceptions to the rule.  As time went on, however, and I saw this dynamic more and more, I was perplexed.

I had always assumed that the most important aspect of being able to teach your child math was to be able to

## Chapter Three: Common Pitfalls

do it *yourself*, really well. The better you were at math, the better you'd be able to teach it, right? Obviously, engineers would be great at teaching math! So why was I seeing so many kids-of-engineers with math dislike and disability? Over time I came to see some commonalities and began to form in my mind an image of the stereotypical "Engineer Dad."

When Engineer Dad homeschools math, everyone has high hopes. Most of the time it works out really well, and the kids get an excellent mathematical education. Sometimes, however, it backfires and the kids end up hating math. Ironically, when Engineer Dad homeschools math, it is quite frequently a *perfect storm* of Haphazard Teaching, Added Confusion, and Unrealistic Expectations.

When he starts out, Engineer Dad is excited about homeschooling, and enthusiastic about teaching his children math. He is confident that he will be able to do this well, since, after all, he *is* a professional. He loves his kids and wants nothing but the best for them.

But Engineer Dad is a pretty busy guy. He's busy with work, busy with the family, busy around the house. He gets tired, he gets cranky, he gets sick. He has to fix the toilet, or he has to fly to Texas. All these things conspire to get in the way of his consistently teaching his kids math. Before he knows it, two weeks have flown by, and there hasn't been any time for math!

But never fear. He said he'd get the job done, and he will! He swoops in, gung-ho! He sits down and enthusiastically starts going over problems. He lectures on and on, way beyond the point where Johnny can concentrate. Engineer Dad feels bad that he hasn't been able to put much time into this math thing lately, so he wants to make up for it and cram it all in now.

Engineer Dad also has a bit of a rough time getting down to Johnny's level. He just assumes that he's good at explaining things because he's good at *doing* them. When Johnny *doesn't* understand him, Engineer Dad thinks Johnny isn't trying. Or worse, he secretly fears that maybe his son is not too bright. Things math-related have always been so clear to E-D, that he can't even see *why* an explanation might be needed! It's clear! It's obvious! He gets frustrated. Somehow, he thought this would be easier.

Sometimes Engineer Dad feels the pressure. He knows he hasn't been able to devote as much time to math as he'd intended, because he's off saving the world so much. He feels guilty. Engineer Dad doesn't mean it, but his guilt often shows itself as frustration at Johnny's lack of progress.

But the biggest problem of all is that Engineer Dad just confuses the *heck* out of little Johnny. E-D is so confident of his own math abilities that he doesn't think he needs to work through any problems on his own before he goes over them with Johnny. He always answers math problems "on the spot." But frequently he will go down one or two wrong roads before taking the correct approach, enthusiastically explaining his thinking all along the way. By the time Engineer Dad gets around to explaining the *correct* approach, Johnny's head is spinning, and he has no idea what is going on.

Other times Engineer Dad just gets so excited! He is *sure* that Johnny wants to hear all the tangents he goes off on. He is sure that Johnny wants to take it "one step further!" Engineer Dad often loses track of what Johnny knows or doesn't know already, and his explanations often go right over Johnny's head.

E-D is also a stereotypical "guy," in that he's not super-emotionally-aware, if you know what I mean. The look of confusion and exhaustion on Johnny's face simply does not register with him, and Engineer Dad just happily talks on and on.

When Johnny has finally had enough and in frustration cries out that he doesn't want Dad's "help" anymore, Engineer Dad is crushed! Poor E-D! He is just trying to help. He really is. His intentions really are good. If only he could come down to Johnny's level, and be a little less "smart" and excited, everything would be OK!

Now, obviously, this is a cartoonish exaggeration! Guys- please don't be offended! I am just trying to illustrate a point. And ladies, before you get too smug, let's admit it. Some of *us* are like this too!

You don't have to be an engineer, or even a *dad*, to be an "Engineer Dad."

Because this unexpected dynamic is so common, I actually suggest that the parent who is *weaker* in math do the teaching, at least in the early years. A "weaker" math parent may be able to relate to his kid better, and understand what is "hard" and why. He is more likely to take his time and prepare well in advance, and to be honestly impressed and proud whenever his kid understands the latest topic. The stronger math parent is more likely to have unrealistic expectations of his child and get quickly frustrated.

You don't have to be an engineer to teach fractions. You *do* have to be able to discern when you are, or are *not*, being understood. You need to be able to read the cues of boredom and frustration, and adjust your approach accordingly. If your child is not "getting it," you have to be able to examine your own approach and adjust it, instead of assuming the fault lays with your child. It doesn't. More important than being "good" at math, is being able to communicate with your child. You have to be a good listener, as much as a good explainer. How will you know *what* to explain if you can't really listen and hear what the issue is?

When a child is taught math by a parent that is good at math and it doesn't work out well, everyone just assumes that the child is not good at math, instead of considering that the parent might not be so good at teaching it. If Dad, who is an engineer, is getting frustrated with Johnny because he isn't "getting" what he is telling him, of *course* Johnny is going to think that he's no good at math. *Dad's* the professional after all! Feeling confused is a horrible feeling. Having your parent frustrated with you is worse. Having both together is something any normal child would try to avoid. It's no wonder that some of these kids reject math.

## The Unschooling Approach

While Engineer Dad may get overly intense and excited about math, some parents go to the opposite extreme and will sit back and wait for their child to show some interest before teaching him any math.

One of my favorite things about homeschooling is that we parents can focus more on the things our kids are interested in, and less on the things they don't care about. Many homeschool families, in fact, study *only* whatever the kids show an active interest in. While I don't completely take this unschooling approach, I really do love the idea of it, and do incorporate aspects of it into my own personal homeschool philosophy. Many of these unschooled kids end up very happy and absolutely brilliant in one area or another!

These kids often eventually do want to learn math when they decide that they want to go to college to study Music Theory or something like that. They discover that they need at least basic math skills in order to be accepted to the school they want to go to, and suddenly they are motivated like never before!

I *have* known several homeschoolers who were terribly behind in math like this, and then became motivated, caught up and even excelled at math. It can and does happen, and homeschoolers certainly have a better chance of turning it around than anyone.

However, these are the exceptions. What *usually* happens is that these kids never do catch up. Sometimes they feel like they are so far behind that they will never catch up, so what's the point? By the time they realize that math skills really *would* be useful to them, they often feel like it is too late, or that it is too much work to catch up. This really is something to think about: Whenever you do start, it *is* going to take a certain amount of time to progress through all the topics.

So yes, you *can* get around to studying math later, but you are taking a bit of a chance. Even our wonderfully super-socialized homeschool teens are self-conscious at times and crave acceptance and approval from their peers. Like anyone else, they can become embarrassed by their lack of skill at something that all their friends seem to have down pat. This can then make them unwilling to even try.

## Creative Math

Many homeschool families, like Laura's, are well-educated and quite aware that math can and *should* be creative and fun. They totally understand that math is a wonderfully

...ng field. Perhaps they have seen pictures of frac... heard of Chaos Theory. Unfortunately, many of these families often reject what they consider to be the "boring" nuts and bolts of math education, don't spend enough time on the basics, and their kids never even *get* to the really creative stuff!

It's like trying to read Tolstoy with a 2$^{nd}$ grade vocabulary. It's just not going to happen, no matter how much you like the *idea* of it. Or like wanting them to play a piano concerto without ever having put in those years of work on the basics. Learning the basics doesn't have to be drudgery, but it does have to happen!

Math is a foreign language. Some really interesting ideas are much better expressed in this language than in English. What we might never be able to easily describe in English can be expressed clearly and concisely in math. Unless you speak the language, you don't have much of a chance of understanding these ideas.

Parents who want their children to appreciate art really should take the time to educate their kids in math. There are so many beautiful mathematical ideas out there, and when you can understand one and see what it is saying, it touches you in the same way that art or music do. Many of us think of math as a dull and practical skill, but much of it is just as "impractical" as any art! The ideas are just beautiful, on their own, *without purpose.* Real mathematicians are more like artists than you might imagine.

Many people can listen to and enjoy a piece of music, even if they haven't studied music theory or can't play an instrument. If you really "know" music you will probably get more out of a concerto, but others, like me, can still enjoy it. I don't know classical music at all – I barely know a tenor from a soprano – but when my friend Stephanie takes me to the opera, I still have a good time. On the hand, a beautiful piece of math, a "Math Work of Art," if you may, is usually completely inaccessible to people with poor math skills, and reading or hearing it is not enjoyable at all.

If we don't understand math well we will not be able to follow the logic of a beautifully creative idea or technique. We won't be able to enjoy the discussion on some lower level, the way that we can with music or art. We either will "get it" or not. If we do get it, it's a beautiful thing. If we don't, then the whole conversation was wasted time for us.

Truth is stranger than fiction, and the world is a wonderfully mysterious place. Math is a wonderful language in which to express many strange truths. When you can speak the language of math, this only becomes more clear. If you ever want to be blown away, look up Benford's Law, and its applications in law enforcement.

If you want your kid to enjoy the creativity of math, he <u>has</u> to understand the basics. It doesn't have to involve hours of isolation, or angry battles. It doesn't have to be drudgery. But it does have to happen!

## Warning: Contentious Material Ahead!

Now, you may find this hard to believe, but one of the biggest obstacles I see to kids' developing good, solid math skills is their parents declaring them "gifted." I personally think that the word gifted is over-used and watered down. Most kids who are categorized as gifted, either by their parents or by a school, are, in my opinion, just healthy, bright kids.

I'm not saying these kids are not smart. I would just like to leave the term "gifted" to those very, very few who truly deserve it! In fact, I can honestly say that I've only ever had one student that I truly felt was gifted. The rest of them, my own boys included, are just healthy, happy, normal, bright kids!

Many people think that it improves a kid's self esteem to be called gifted. I suppose the idea is that he will rise to the level of expectation. If that were always true, I'd be all for it.

However, in my experience, being labeled gifted can actually have a negative impact on your child's math education. Many parents of "gifted" children push them into math that is way too hard for them, which just confuses them and actually causes them to fall behind. These parents, *and I see them all the time*, hear about the latest math book that "everyone" is using. They decide that since their child is "gifted," he's got to be at least two years ahead in math! Because he is declared "gifted," it is an absolute, unthinkable possibility that he do math work at grade-level. This is a set-up for failure and low self-esteem, and unfortunately I have seen it a lot.

These kids, who really *are* smart, get confused and overwhelmed, and actually <u>fall behind</u> in math. All because their parents decided that they should do algebra in 5th grade! That seems like a terrible waste. I have seen many "average" kids bypass by these "gifted" kids simply because they were consistently taught to the appropriate level.

Another problem I see with kids being labeled "gifted" and taking it too much to heart, is that they try to avoid making mistakes at all costs. And math is *all* about making mistakes! There are *way* more mistakes than correct answers in math. Mistakes are awesome – they are how we learn. Some kids are mortified if they blurt out a wrong answer. Often they are so mortified that they can barely listen to the correct explanation. <u>To succeed at math, you</u>

absolutely *have* to be able to make mistakes and still <u>good about yourself</u>. Not the same silly mistake over, a͟ ͟ over, but different ones, new ones, all over the place. No matter how smart we are, if we are ashamed of our mistakes, learning math will be a horrible experience.

Many kids who are labeled "gifted" also really glory in their title. Why wouldn't they? They get lots of praise and attention for it, so of *course* the label is important to them. Often these kids won't ask questions because they don't want to display any shred of ignorance. They never get their questions answered, which does them a disservice. At other times they are so busy trying to display their awesome knowledge that they can't stop to listen and learn.

Ironically, many kids who are labeled "gifted" will reject math, because it is very much a "Put your Money where your Mouth is" endeavor. We all have a tendency to want to only do those things that we know we can do well, and to avoid things we might fail at. Rather than take the chance that they are not math geniuses, many "gifted" kids will simply claim that they "don't like math," so that their academic superiority goes unchallenged and untested.

By labeling a child "gifted," we are making education a competitive game, and we are declaring our kids champions. Champions have to constantly defend their titles – unless they give up the sport and retire early! None of us parents wants our kids to "retire early" from math. Not *this* early.

In spite of the best intentions, by labeling a child "gifted" many parents add elements of fear, stress and competition to their child's educational atmosphere. From what I've seen, it does way more harm than good.

If you have a bright child, who really is doing math work that is way above grade-level, the suggestions in this book are especially important. If she enjoys math, and you want to continue to foster that, then she will need even more of your time and attention. Don't assume that her time management, note-taking or *frustration-management* skills are in line with her math skills. Many bright kids will be ready for advanced math concepts way before they are ready to read a math book to themselves, or manage their own time and progress.

CHAPTER FOUR
# THE ALGEBRA 1 & GEOMETRY YEARS

If you have already been following the suggestions in this book for the earlier years, you are in great shape. With a couple of tweaks here and there, you will just want to continue what you've already been doing. However, if you are just starting to teach math to your child, because either he just started homeschooling, or after a couple of non-math years, take heart! It is not too late for you to jump in with both feet, brush up on your skills and make that decision to take your math Full-Contact.

If your child has already learned how to solve simple equations in Pre-Algebra, then you could do either Geometry or Algebra 1 next. Algebra 1 is usually taught before Geometry, but the actual algebra skills used in Geometry are pretty simple. Most kids know them before they even start Algebra 1. 90% of what you learn in Algebra 1 won't show up in Geometry, but Algebra 2 follows directly and logically from Algebra 1. If you stick an entire year of Geometry in between Algebra 1 and 2, your kid will have a whole year to not-use and forget everything that he worked hard to learn in Algebra 1. I taught my kids Algebra 1 and Geometry at the same time, but if I were to go back and do one *after* the other, I would definitely do Geometry first.

## Some Thoughts on Algebra 1

Algebra 1, and the mastery of its concepts, is vital for continued success in Mathematics. Without a really solid foundation in Algebra 1, the subsequent math courses of Algebra 2, Pre-Calculus and Calculus will be a real struggle. If your kid wants to go any further in math, he absolutely *must* master Algebra 1.

A traditional Algebra 1 course focuses mainly on equations of straight lines, or "Linear Functions," which represent direct relationships. Even very young kids understand the idea of the hourly wage: If I make $5/hour, then the more I work, the more I earn. There is a *direct* relationship between how much we work, and how much we earn. This type of direct relationship is the number one focus of Algebra 1. We learn how to express that relationship in the language of math. This is called an equation. We then also learn how to draw a picture that describes this relationship, and we call it a graph.

In Algebra 1 we study, in great detail, how to go back and forth between these different ways of describing this type of direct relationship: with words, with symbols and numbers, and with a picture. We learn how to draw the graph from the equation; how to write the equation from the graph; how to start with English and end up with a graph; how to start with a graph and interpret the English meaning. Backward, forward, up, down and sideways, until we hardly know what we are doing anymore!

It's easy to lose sight of the fact that these are just three different ways of saying the same simple thing, and that all we are learning to do is to go back and forth among them.

The picture of these types of relationships is always going to be a straight line, the equation is always going to

## Chapter FOUR: The Algebra 1 & Geo...

have two variables, and the English is al[...] describing a direct relationship. Having [...] the same thing may seem like overkill, but [...] find it to be useful.

Making things in Algebra 1 even more [...] fact that, once your picture or your word [...]ption is finally translated into Math, there then seem to be a million different ways of writing the equation. A million *equivalent-but-different* ways of saying the same exact thing! This is true. Even in math, the language of the engineer and the accountant, there are many, many ways to say exactly the same thing!

So *within* the language of math itself, you may have to express your very simple relationship in one of various "famous" ways: Standard Form, Slope-Intercept Form or Point-Slope Form, for example. They are all *absolutely* equivalent, but sometimes you want to say it one way, sometimes another. Sometimes you want your X on the left; sometimes you want it on the right! Just like in English, sometimes the Blunt Comment is most useful, and at other times the Subtle Hint might be more appropriate. Who knew that mathematicians were so sensitive? They are!

So, basically, Algebra 1 is The Line or The Direct Relationship, in excruciating, painstaking detail. You are learning how to express your thoughts about direct relationships verbally, mathematically, and pictorially. This is the number one big idea of Algebra 1.

However, a traditional Algebra 1 course will also throw in some new types of arithmetic that your kid may not have seen before. She will learn about things called "exponents" and "radicals." Just when your child is getting comfortable with equations, the focus will shift onto *snippets* of equations, called expressions. I like to think of an equation as a

...ce, and an expression as a phrase or a clause. Just ...here are different formats for an entire equation, there are also different, (yet equivalent!), ways of writing your expression.

Algebra 1 courses love to insist on specific formats for your expressions. They have decided that one way is called "simplified," even if it looks more complicated! For example, it is never OK to have a square root sign in the bottom of a fraction. Mathematically, it really makes no difference, but boy, is it bad manners!

I think one reason for this is that it makes grading tests and homework easier for teachers if everyone puts his answer in exactly the same format. However, as much as it may seem silly and contrived, learning how to "simplify" really is good practice in expressing the same thing in various ways. This really *will* be useful as time goes on. Believe it or not, sometimes you really will want $2/4$ instead of $1/2$.

Toward the end of the course, most Algebra 1 texts will introduce you to your first curvy line, show you how it is the same and different from the Straight Line, and teach you how to apply all your newly acquired skills to it. This is an Algebra 2 teaser, if you will. Most Algebra 2 texts will start by going back and reviewing the Straight Line, before going on to talk about every possible variation of curvy line, and their real world applications.

If your child is currently struggling with Algebra 1, my first guess is that he has not mastered some aspects of his arithmetic. When students come to me for help with Algebra 1, they overwhelmingly have trouble with either "Positives and Negatives" or "Fractions." Check those skills first. Then put the textbook aside, and review all the topics leading up to Algebra 1– *together*. It may take a week, or it may take months, but it will be well worth it! Start with the basics, and progress together. Take time to sit together every day and make progress on your review. This is crucial. First it will review her arithmetic for her. Second, it will review yours for *you*, and third it will make math a sit-down-together activity, which will reduce everyone's frustration. But don't forget to keep it short and sweet!

## Some Thoughts on Geometry

Geometry is the math course that has the greatest potential for converting indifferent kids into math lovers. It is fun, easy to conceptualize and doesn't generally involve horrible long algebraic equations. Each idea is short, sweet, obvious and practical. Honestly, an average fifth-grader could understand the concepts and have fun with them. Geometry problems are puzzles that are fun to solve!

What often happens, in reality, is that Geometry is the course that completely cements a student's deep, deep hatred and disdain for math.

There seems to be a conspiracy among Geometry text writers to make their books as obtuse, abstruse and verbose as possible. Oops - I mean "hard to understand!" The writers seem to be in league together to make easy concepts as incomprehensible as possible, short of writing them in a foreign language. They are like the Wizard of Oz, afraid that we will find out that their ideas are not mystical, magical or inaccessibly difficult.

A traditional Geometry course consists of more English vocabulary than it does math. Things aren't equal, they're *congruent*; they aren't cut in half, they are *bisected*. Why use a simple word when a complicated one will do just as well? On the other hand, you also have innocent-sounding words like "similar" and "regular," very easily overlooked, that convey a whole slew of specific meanings that are *essential* to solving problems.

Geometry is a tool kit of about 50 pretty simple facts. Each one is easy to understand and use, and if you put them together you can do some amazing things. I like to think of Geometry as a toolkit where each fact is a tool to be used as needed. Each tool might be pretty simple, but put them together and you can build a house.

Geometry textbooks will call these facts Theorems, or if they are *really* insecure about their Math-hood, they will call some of them Theorems, some Postulates, and some Corollaries. Each book assigns each fact of Geometry its own cryptically verbose name and official-sounding "Theorem Number." Students are then expected to write down these paragraph-length names as justification for every step in solving problems.

It's not enough to know and to be able to *apply* the ideas of Geometry, students also are required to remember that the particular fact they are using might be called the "Corresponding Parts of Congruent Triangles are Congruent Postulate." I am not kidding! It's not enough to be able to use a hammer, you have to remember to call it a *portative tack implanter*, or maybe an *implement of fustigation*!

School kids definitely have it worse in this area. At least most homeschoolers' tests are open book. We don't have to waste our time and brainpower memorizing all these theorem names. Especially when someone else's book calls it something completely different!

The *ideas* of geometry definitely are important to keep and take into the future with you, but the *names* of those ideas are unimportant. This is not always obvious but, I promise you, it is true. You *should* learn, and remember forever, that opposite angles are equal. You *don't* need to remember that the particular fact is called the Vertical Angle Congruence Theorem, or whatever *your* book decides to call it.

If you cut through all the "verbose verbiage," there really is just not that much _to_ Geometry. For many kids, spending an entire year on Geometry is a waste of time. The concepts are all simple enough for a fifth-grader to understand, and can often be learned in a couple of months. For others it can and should be a relatively relaxing and enjoyable math year.

## Approaches for Both Algebra 1 and Geometry

Before you get started with either Algebra 1 or Geometry, you have to know for sure that your child is ready for it, or you will be setting him up for failure. You could give him one of the many placement tests that are out there, but you have to be sure that you know how to interpret the results. These test results can mean different things for different kids. For one kid, an 80% can mean "mastery of concepts with some silly mistakes thrown in", while for another it means that he has only learned 8 of each 10 things he needs to know. The difference is important!

Placement tests are excellent, in that they give you a guide to which topics are considered pre-requisites for a course. Just make sure that you take a good look at any problems your kid gets wrong, and make sure it was just a silly mistake, or go back and learn the material. Also, beware of multiple choice tests! Guessing is a *huge* problem in math, and guessing correctly can mask some serious gaps in knowledge. If you have a placement test that you want to give your kid, and it is multiple choice, I'd suggest blacking out all the choices. He should be able to come up with the right answer himself, without a list of answers to pick from. **M-C Tests are only popular b/c they are easy to grade!**

❈ ❈ ❈

Whether you decide to do Algebra 1 or Geometry first, or both of them together, all of the suggestions from the previous chapter still apply. First, you have to brush up your *own* math skills. Then make a point to *never* put work in front of him that you can't quickly and easily help him with. Third, take your math Full-Contact.

Brushing up on your own math skills is vital at this stage. So too is taking the time, on your own, to work through all the problems you want to assign to him ahead of time. Whenever he gets stuck, your kid really needs you to be right there to give him quick, clear answers and guidance. And he will get stuck a lot. There is simply no learning math without getting stuck. It's just what happens. If your kid can't get good, quick help from you whenever he gets stuck, he may get frustrated and give up.

The Algebra 1 and Geometry years are possibly the time when your kid needs you the most. The ideas and the problems are much more challenging than ever before. For many kids, this is a time of frustration, and they can spend the whole year barely having any idea of what's going on. I have seen many, many kids who are getting decent "grades" in Algebra 1, but who absolutely have no idea what's happening. This comes back to haunt them later when they really need to be able to use and apply this material.

I know it sounds like a lot of work, and it is. However, if you do this stage right, then the next stage will be so much easier and take a lot less of your time and energy. In fact, for many parents, this can be the *last* big super-involved year. Next year their kids will be mature enough and have a good enough foundation to get through Algebra 2 either on their own, via an online course, or at a community college.

This is the make it or break it time. If there is ever a time to drop everything and do math with your kid, this is it!

## Permission to watch TV

Video tutorials are a great tool. Even if you are using one single curriculum, I would strongly suggest watching supplemental video lessons that correspond to what your child is learning. There are some excellent ones out there. While you might not want to use them as your main math text, I would absolutely suggest that you use them as reinforcement. During the Algebra 1 years, my boys and I watched many videos that I had chosen to correspond with what we were learning.

It is impossible to know, without previously watching it yourself, whether a video is going to be accessible and interesting to your child or not. The title "Graphing Equations" doesn't tell you how easy or hard it is. I strongly suggest that you preview all the videos before you sit down together. Reducing the potential for frustration is one of our main goals!

## The Dreaded Textbook

Math textbooks can definitely be challenging to read and understand. If you are using one main textbook for this phase, then now is an excellent time to start teaching your child exactly *how to read a math book*. Most of us, as soon as we open a math book, get instant ADD. We expect to be able to read the math book as quickly as we read a novel, and when we can't, our eyes start jumping all over the page.

Believe it or not, many math books are actually quite readable, and have really good explanations, – but you have to have patience! You have to lower your *time* expectations, and take it slowly. Take your time on each and every sentence, and make an *active* effort to follow their logic. Math books cannot be "passively read" the way we read a novel in the evening. They take active, conscious effort to read. It is a mental workout, which gets easier with practice. When we expect to be able to read through a math book breezily, we get frustrated and disappointed. However, when we *expect* it to be slow and laborious, and decide to do it anyway, we are often pleasantly surprised!

Ideally, throughout the course, you will be staying one step ahead of your child. You should be reading the book by yourself before you sit down to read it with her. Read it slowly. See if it makes sense to *you*. It should. You should read through the entire section and work out at least some of the problems before you even think about sitting down with your child. When you feel confident that you yourself *do* understand the new section, you can read the book together. Reading the book out loud together is an excellent practice. Take your time, and frequently pause to make sure she is following the logic.

What you are doing here is teaching your kid *how to read a math book*. This is a seriously underrated and underdeveloped skill. Most of us read the first sentence or two, then skip to the example problem and try to figure it out. There is something about actually reading a math book that makes our minds go blank. And kids are generally even more impatient than we are. If they can't just glance quickly at the page and "know" it, they often give up. By reading

*Chapter FOUR: The Algebra 1 & Geometry Years*

the book together out loud you are bringing his expectations *in line with reality* by showing him that reading a page of a math book is *supposed* to take a long time.

This may seem hard and tedious, but this is a skill: a skill that definitely becomes easier with practice. It takes a bit of determination at first, especially if you are unsure of your own ability to understand it. That's why you go off and work on it by yourself first.

If you truly *can't* follow the logic in your textbook, and have no idea what it is asking you for, there are a couple of things to consider. First, you could look up the same topic in another book, in a video series, or even online. Nothing in Algebra 1 or Geometry is unique, and in spite of what people may say, there is no "new" math. $2 + 2 = 4$ no matter what book you read. The techniques and ideas introduced in Algebra 1 are "famous" and you should easily be able to find a good description of each topic somewhere.

If, after looking all over, you still can't figure it out, maybe go back a couple of chapters to see if there was anything you missed. If you glossed over or forgot something, that might be the problem.

Another thing to consider is that, every now and then, a textbook might throw a completely unrelated topic in the mix, at some seemingly arbitrary point. Maybe they are trying to keep it interesting, but are just ending up being confusing. Maybe the topic is not critical to your continuing on with the book, and you can just skip it.

If, after all this, your textbook is still incomprehensible, then you might just want to get a better book! There are plenty of good books out there, and if you look around, you will be sure to find one that works for you.

※ ※ ※

I didn't start reading math textbooks consistently with Alex until he took Algebra 2. Before then we had been using a bunch of different books and videos. Then for Algebra 2 we started using one of those big, traditional textbooks. I felt like the reading in the text was too hard for him to do easily on his own, but I did want him to follow the logic, so I would read the book out loud to him, as he followed along.

One great thing about using one single curriculum is that you gain a familiarity with your book's way of presenting things. You get to know your book, so it actually gets easier to read with time. This definitely happened for us. One day, as we were near the end of the course, I was busy and couldn't sit with Alex and do math. I told him to go do some other school work. Since he would generally rather do math than any other subject, he decided to try it on his own. He was able to sit, read and follow the next section all by himself, without needing or wanting my help. That was when I realized that he had learned how to read and comprehend his textbook, and that it was a valuable and *acquirable* skill. All that reading together time had paid off! This is what we are all striving for.

Even though I started doing it later, in Algebra 2, if you are using one text consistently, I do suggest you start reading it aloud together now. Your goal is for your child to be able to do this on his own at some point, comfortably teaching himself. Even if he eventually goes back to school, or takes his math courses at a local community college, this will be an extremely valuable skill.

I didn't follow a specific curriculum for either of my boys at this stage of their math development. I just went topic

## Chapter FOUR: The Algebra 1 & Geometry Years

to topic, moving on whenever it felt right, using whichever books or videos worked. It ended up, without my planning for it, that Algebra 1 and Geometry topics were covered in the same year.

When my boys were each in fifth grade, they learned about simple equations. They knew the arithmetic basics by then. They thought equations were cool, and knowing how to solve them allowed us to start doing some more fun problems. Fifth grade was all about arithmetic, fractions, percents, and very simple equations. Toward the end of that year I taught them to solve "two-equations with two variables." I only showed them one way to do it so that they didn't get confused by the several ways that are usually taught. I emphasized to them that math is a foreign language and I spent a *lot* of time teaching them how to translate from English to math. For the next year or so I mostly did a mish-mosh of various problems. I picked and chose problems from various books, whatever looked interesting.

I did a lot of jumping around in sixth grade. We didn't do any graphing, we didn't do "linear equations." We just did lots and lots of problems! Most days I would just write down five or ten problems for them to do on a clean sheet of paper. Half of the problems might be arithmetic problems, chosen at random: Hmm, let's see. We haven't done anything like, "what is 6% of 250?" in a while, I'll add that! The other half were word problems, either copied from a book or made up to suit their current interest. My word problems usually had something to do with guns or explosives or cars at excessive speeds. Go figure!

And that's it. That is pretty much what we did that entire year. We sat down for about 15 minutes of math each day *together*. Certainly never longer than that. Honestly, 5 minutes a day was more common at this point. I spent way more time off on my own, staying one step ahead, looking for new problems, or researching good books and videos for us to use. I'm not sure if they learned a lot of *new* stuff that year, but we did do a lot of word problems, and we were constantly revisiting old ideas and techniques. It was during this year that we started watching various interesting or on-topic math videos together, which is one of my very favorite things to do. At this stage I still previewed each and every one, and only showed them ones that I felt they would "get" and enjoy!

My main focus at this stage was for them to enjoy math. We didn't spend tons of time on it, but we did do something math-related practically every day. There was no rote practice, and I switched things up a lot so that they learned how to do problems "out of context." I kept things short and sweet, and only worked while their brains were fully on and focused. If they were tired and draggy, we'd skip it. I kept math a fully-focused, brain-on activity.

None of this was planned; I was always just doing the next thing that presented itself to me that seemed fun, interesting and productive.

By the start of seventh grade Alex was learning about Quadratic Equations. I was looking around for the "next" math thing for him, but I was finding that most of the Algebra books looked pretty dry for a 12-year-old. Someone told me that the Johns Hopkins Gifted program required kids to take the SAT's in seventh grade, so just out of curiosity, I checked out an SAT Math book. Of course, lots of it was stuff Alex had never seen and wasn't ready for. However, to my surprise, much of it actually looked learnable for him, given what he already knew.

Now, as I've said before, I don't think Alex is gifted. He's a normal, healthy, bright boy. The math in the SAT book just looked like more fun than the Algebra books I was investigating. It had lots of geometry, lots of word problems, lots of random thinking-on-your-feet puzzle-problems; lots of out-of-context, thinking problems as opposed to pages and pages of rote practice.  So we got an SAT prep book and set about learning what was in it.  The study guide showed me *which* important basics to master, gave me a brief review of them, and then we used other books and videos to learn things in more depth.

Alex and I spent the first half of seventh grade working on SAT math – we learned lots of cool geometry, how to graph equations, and all sorts of other fun and interesting things.  I signed him up for a January test date, but there was never any pressure for him to take the actual test. I told him from day one that he wouldn't have to take the test if he didn't want to, and that he could change his mind up until the last minute. I meant it, and he believed me. I did not want this to be a "pressure" thing for him.

On the other hand, I *did* insist that he try.  I always tell my boys that it's OK to be bad at stuff, but it's not OK to not *try*! So for that first half of seventh grade, we probably did a good solid half-hour together a day. I'd teach him new stuff or we would go over problems together.  This was also the first time that Alex went off to do some math on his own. Every few days he would do a practice section in his book, and then we'd go over it together.  I myself took each and every practice section before I assigned it to him.  That way I *knew* what I was asking of him, and I knew how to help him on the problems he could not get.

Without planning to, by working through the SAT book, we had covered the highlights of Algebra 1 and Geometry in one fell swoop! I liked this approach so much that I followed the same approach with Scott.  Both boys took the

SATs when they were in 7th grade, each one getting better than 600 on the math section.

For my family this approach worked really well. My boys didn't spend have to spend a year studying "The Line," not seeing the forest for the trees. They didn't have to learn the "Supplementary Angles Congruency Theorem." They just had to learn the math. That SAT study guide told me *what* to learn then we set about figuring out *how* to learn it.

We did Algebra 1 and Geometry at the same time, under the guise of SAT prep. I like this approach, and highly recommend it. When I started this with Alex, I hadn't intended to skip these courses; I figured he'd get to them at some point when he was more mature. However, when I revisited those courses, I realized that he had already covered all of Algebra 1 and Geometry, and was well-prepared to go on to Algebra 2.

One of the biggest benefits of this approach was the out-of-context abilities that the boys developed. They were constantly switching gears, using different techniques and tools, never knowing what ideas or techniques might be needed, so they had to keep them all mentally available. They didn't get trained to only consider those techniques that were being taught in the current chapter.

## But I Don't Have Time for This!

The Algebra 1 and Geometry stage is a pivotal phase in your child's math development, and the one in which you want to be most involved. If your child gets lost here, he won't be able to go any further. Kids often reach Algebra 1 and Geometry before they are mature enough to work independently, stay focused, manage their frustration, or

## Chapter FOUR: The Algebra 1 & Geometry Years

struggle through something they don't understand, and this is why they need our help.

Some parents really cannot put all this time and energy into their child's math at this point. I get that. Life gets busy, throws us curveballs. We don't have time, or we really don't feel capable. What I have outlined above is *ideal*, but there <u>are</u> other options.

In the next chapter I will discuss the role of math tutors in your child's education. However, for many of us private tutoring is simply not an option. What do we do then? If we can't teach it ourselves, and we can't afford a tutor, what on Earth can we do?

First of all, relax. Continue to do math at whatever level your child is currently at. Keep it fun, short and sweet, but <u>consistent</u>. Five or ten problems a day, ten minutes or so, just to maintain and reinforce what he already knows. Get videos on topics he already knows. Let the math he already knows get stronger and stronger. Don't let him get rusty: periodically have him add two fractions or find a percent. Sit with him for those ten minutes each day. This I *know* you can do.

Then just wait. He will mature. He will soon be ready to take an Algebra 1 course either online or at a community college. You will know when he's ready: just make sure you really *do* wait until he is. He will need to be mature enough to ask his teachers for help, and to recognize when he needs it. He will have to be able to work independently. But most of all, he will have to be <u>willing</u>. If he is unwilling, all you will hear about is how the book stinks and the teacher hates him. Since he will be doing the course independently, how will you know if this is true? (It usually isn't!) He is much more likely to be willing if he has a good math attitude, and solid, basic arithmetic skills. These are what you should be working on maintaining now.

If he is 13 and you push him to work through an Algebra 1 course on his own now, before he is really ready, and without much support from you, he may get lost and confused and negative. If he goes on to do more math after that, he will not do as well as he otherwise might have. Why not wait a year, or even <u>two</u>? At fifteen or sixteen, he'll be a whole different creature! If he has a good math-attitude, and has kept up with his arithmetic skills, then at that point he'll whiz through Algebra 1 in no time.

It is a scary thing to wait, but it is much better than pushing him and confusing him. <u>Confusion is really, really hard to undo</u>.

Remember, math builds on itself. The foundation has to be strong. It is better to wait and be able to build the next layer well, rather than to build it poorly, and then build on top of that. Resist the urge to want him to be learning "something." Doing that is very often worse than doing nothing at all.

CHAPTER FIVE
# MATH TUTORING

Many families assume that if they hire a tutor for their child, everything will just work out fine. That may be, and it may not be. Of course, I *have* seen cases where tutoring helped tremendously, but I have also seen many cases where it made little or no difference. Just like with a textbook, it is how you *use* tutoring that counts.

## Tutoring for Arithmetic/Pre-Algebra Phase

I don't usually recommend tutoring for kids in the arithmetic or pre-algebra phase. First of all, most tutoring sessions are an hour, and most of these kids do not yet have the capability to concentrate for that long. Second, your child really needs to be doing math *every day*, even if just for a few minutes, and who is going to help her when she gets stuck during the week? Third, math then becomes just another thing to "fit in," not something you share together. And lastly, tutoring is expensive! Take the money that you would have spent and have someone clean your home while you yourself brush up on your math – or just go and have some fun with it!

Worst of all, you are missing the opportunity to do math with your child – to demonstrate with your actions that math is important and compelling. If *you* don't want to do math, how can you convince *her* that it is interesting and worthwhile? If you tell her that you can't remember how to do it, and she sees you not even *trying* to remember, how can you ask her to put in the effort? This is especially true for mothers and their daughters. At this stage, no matter your background or skill level, you really are her best math teacher!

Once you make that decision that you yourself are really going to do this – that you are going to sit down with those books and give it a go yourself – I promise you it won't be as hard as you think!

If you really are overwhelmed and feel that you can't possibly re-teach yourself arithmetic, then here are a couple choices. Get a tutor for her at *least* two or three times a week, for a *short* session and you sit in on the sessions, so that you learn the material as well. You can also take notes, and remember clearly what was taught in the session. This will be good for both of you, and math will now be a "together" activity. When your child gets stuck on a problem during the week, <u>which she will</u>, you are far more likely to remember what the tutor said than your child is.

Another alternative would be for just you, the parent, to get tutored. As you master each concept, you can then teach it to your kid. This will be much cheaper, because you will learn very quickly on your own. It will definitely be more productive because the tutor will be focused just on you. Also, you will probably find that once a tutor gets you started, you are soon able to make progress on your own.

Remember, your child needs to be doing *short sessions of math frequently.* If you do get a tutor just once a week, your child will really need to be doing problems on the other days. She will really also need good, quick help to be available to her on those days, and that help will have to be you!

Many homeschool families first consider hiring a tutor during the pre-algebra years. Maybe they have let math go a little, and they are concerned. Usually these parents feel that their kids are "behind" and they feel pressured.

The Swansons were a family just like this. Dad was a scientist, so they had just assumed math was "taken care of" – he would teach his daughter himself. But it just hadn't happened. Life got in the way, and by 7th grade Eloise was "behind." They came to me for tutoring, and I started to work with her every week.

Eloise *was* behind, I suppose, but also extremely bright. I initially had no concerns about getting her up to speed. She had a great attitude, and picked things up pretty quickly. Her parents seemed very involved and concerned, so I was optimistic.

My optimism drained away, however, as the weeks went on. Each week I would prepare daily problem sets for her to do during the week. Short and sweet 10-minute reinforcements of what we had talked about. They were *never* done. Not once did she come back to me with all five of her daily sets completed, each one done on a different day. The closest she came was doing three of them, all in a row, right before she came to see me.

Every week I urged Eloise and her mother to try to do this consistently. Every week they said they would, and every week they didn't. Eloise's mom was upset with her for not doing them, but she was giving her daughter *no* help, guidance or structure.

Sometimes Eloise said she was just too busy. Sometimes she had forgotten how to do something, and even though I had told her that she could call me if that happened, she never did. Eloise's mom was leaving the management of her homework completely up to her.

Parents often become even more hands-off when their kids are being tutored. It is almost as if parents think, "Whew, I'm glad math is someone else's responsibility!" and they become less involved than ever. Only the most motivated kid at this stage will do his daily math without being "made" to do it – and that kid probably doesn't need a math tutor!

If your tutor does assign work to be done during the week, which she should, then you need to create time and space for that to happen. Daily, *not* all at once right before the next appointment! Otherwise you are simply throwing your money away, and even worse, your child will not make any progress.

Another problem with tutoring is that it can add chaos to an already hectic and stressful schedule. Eloise's math appointments were squeezed into a very crowded schedule, and she was generally rushing in and rushing out. It is much more productive to be calm and relaxed when sitting down to learn math, as well as right before and after sessions. This stuff has to percolate and sink in. Constant distractions and busyness will crowd the math out. Frequently this "too-busyness" is the biggest obstacle to learning math, and tutoring just makes it worse!

Eloise was just one of many kids who come to me, who rush out the door each week after tutoring, and never even *think* the word "math" again until the following appointment! Their heads are so full of activities, friends and drama that the math never has a chance to get absorbed. Eloise's appointments generally consisted of me showing her some stuff, her happily "getting it", doing some, then her promptly <u>throwing it in the mental trash can</u> as she walked out the door.

## Tutoring for the Algebra 1 and Geometry Years

At the Algebra 1 and Geometry stage of your child's math development, tutoring really can start to be a useful tool. How you approach it, however, depends not so much on the level of math your child is doing, but on his level of maturity.

If your child is studying Algebra 1 or Geometry at a very young age, read the previous section. Everything there applies to him. Just because he is in a more advanced math course does *not* mean that he has the maturity to complete his assignments unbidden, the ability to take good notes, or even the ability to remember clearly what was said by a tutor three days ago. He will still feel frustration during the week if he gets stuck and no one is available to help him.

Fourteen seems to be a pivotal age for a lot of kids academically. I have seen a lot of kids, once completely disorganized and unable to sit still, change and grow at this age. Kids who before needed to be constantly redirected back to their work start to develop some "staying power." They can manage their frustration better, and put something off and get back to it later. At this age I see kids *starting* to remember their own assignments and to take responsibility and initiative – just starting.

I had one student, Brandon, who was 15, taking a homeschool course equivalent to Algebra 1. Tutoring helped him tremendously, mostly because of how he and his family managed it. First of all, he was at the right level of math.

He had challenges, but was not overwhelmed. Like anyone else, he would forget stuff, but for the most part he was well-prepared by his earlier course work.

When Brandon was younger, his mom had always sat with him and helped him when he got stuck, but at the point that she hired me, she no longer had the time. Not only was the math more challenging, but there were now six younger siblings that she was busy with!

Now that she was more hands-off, Brandon's mom didn't really know *why* he was getting so many of his problems wrong. So she hired me. Someone who could quickly and easily see what he's getting stuck on and what needs to happen. At our first meeting Brandon brought a bunch of exercises he'd been working on over the previous months, and we went over the ones he had gotten wrong. Over 70% were silly mistakes, and the rest were genuine comprehension issues.

After that first meeting with Brandon, I gave his mom a strategy. I told her to make him re-do every problem he gets wrong. There were two reasons for this. First, he would see whether it was just a silly mistake. If it was, then he and I wouldn't need to waste his time and her money going over it. Second, this rule would actually *prevent* silly mistakes from happening in the first place. Most mistakes come from rushing. But when kids know that they might have to do the whole problem over again, just because of one silly mistake, they tend to slow down a bit and be more careful!

Then I suggested that during the week Brandon collect all of the problems that he still got wrong, or just didn't understand. Those would be the problems he and I would work on.

And, believe it or not, this is what he did. Week after week, he would come to me armed with problems he genuinely got stuck on. We would go over them, and our time together was very productive. He progressed quickly through the topics. Even though he seemed like a very mature young man, I am quite convinced that his mother was staying on top of him to *some* degree. It paid off; his preparedness and his consistency were a huge factor in his success.

So tutoring at the Algebra 1 and Geometry stage can really be beneficial. It really all depends on how you manage it. Another choice at this stage is to have your child take a community college or online high school course. They can be a little pricey, but are certainly less than costly private tutoring. The online high school classes, while not providing face-to-face contact, will usually have a teacher that your kid can email back and forth with, who will have online, whiteboard office-hours. If your kid is well-prepared for the course by having mastered the prerequisites, and you are willing to help him with the logistics of an online course, this can be an excellent choice.

## The Winning Strategy for Tutoring

Many families do successfully use tutoring to teach their kids math. Looking at the families I have seen it work for, I can see some commonalities. First, their kids are all placed in an appropriate level of math and they *all* have good math attitudes. None of them is a "reluctant learner." Consistent time is made for math during the week, assignments are always done, and they are always brought back in to go over. Books, pencils and calculators are not forgotten, and appointments are not constantly being cancelled. In every case it is obvious that the parents are overseeing these things, and that they are quite involved. Lastly, none of these families is "too busy," so scheduling tutoring appointments is not adding stress to their lives.

The Full-Contact approach is definitely more productive, rewarding and cost-effective than private tutoring. However, if that can't fit into your life, private tutoring, managed well, can be an excellent alternative.

CHAPTER SIX
# ALGEBRA 2, PRE-CALCULUS, CALCULUS & MORE

So Algebra 1 is basically a whole year on "The Straight Line." We spend an entire year talking about direct relationships, going back and forth among math, English and picture representations.

Algebra 2 takes all those skills, and applies them now to a bunch of other, more complex relationships. Where the picture of the direct relationship was a straight line graph, now the pictures are every variation of curvy that you can imagine. If Algebra 1 is <u>The Straight Line</u>, then Algebra 2 is <u>The World's Most Famous Curvy Lines.</u>

Just as the straight line represents the direct relationship, like the relationship between Hours Worked and Total Salary, these *new* types of lines describe other important and real situations in our world. We now call these relationships "functions." Some of these functions describe profit and loss; some describe population growth; some describe sound. They are all real and useful ways to look at more complex relationships.

Algebra 2 is a pretty hard course. The problems are longer and more complicated than ever. Just as in Algebra 1, some new types of arithmetic are introduced here. Some of these, like "matrices" and "imaginary numbers," are tricky and many kids struggle with them.

But the biggest challenge I see with Algebra 2 is the amount of *detail*. Because we are learning about each function in such detail, and there is so *much* new information to master, it is often hard to see the forest for the trees. In the same way that we want to develop our "number sense" when we are taking arithmetic, in Algebra 2 we want to keep our eye on the big picture, and develop "function sense."

One of the main things that your child will want to take out of an Algebra 2 course is a familiarity with the main types of functions. He should be able to see a picture of a function, and have a general idea of which *type* it is, and the math equation that corresponds to it, and of the real-world type of situation it might apply to. Many kids are so overwhelmed by the details that they can never step back and see the big picture.

Again, a traditional Algebra 2 course is pretty hard. However, it is also a standard requirement at most high schools, so many homeschoolers will want to take it as well. It is vital that your kid is fully prepared before starting this course. This course is challenging enough when you *are* prepared. Going into it with a shaky background is a recipe for disaster.

If you have been teaching your child math Full-Contact up until this point, then obviously the best approach is for you to continue what you are doing. Your child's sessions will get longer, according to his maturity, but he can work on his own more. He can now wait for you to help him when you are ready, without getting overly frustrated. If you have been reading math textbooks together before now, he can probably do that on his own now too. However, you still have to stay one chapter ahead of him. You also still have to go over, on your own, all the problems

*Chapter Six: Algebra 2, Pre-Calculus, Calculus & More*

he needs help with, so that you can help him quickly and effectively without adding to the confusion.

Outside tutoring can be really beneficial at this point, both because many parents feel overwhelmed by this material, and also because the kids are older and able to get more out of it. Before you run out and hire someone, however, be sure to read the previous chapter on how to get the most out of tutoring, because how you manage it makes a big difference!

Community college or online high-school courses are another great option for this stage and above. Like I discussed in the previous section, they will have teachers available for help and are much more affordable than private tutoring. Like the community colleges, many online high schools are accredited, and you can get a recognized high school credit for completing their course. If your kid is college-bound, this may be important. Many schools are skeptical of homeschoolers' math abilities, and you will want to be able to prove your child's skills to them. Like it or not, an accredited grade holds a lot more weight than does your word!

On a related topic, I am a real advocate of homeschoolers taking standardized math tests. First of all, it is just more proof that your kid knows his stuff. Secondly, in preparing for the standardized test, your kid will have to not only know his math, but he will have to be able to *use* it out of context. It's easy to know a graph is going to be exponential if that's the chapter you are on in the book. Not so easy when all the topics are mixed up in order. I think this out-of-context thinking is extremely important and under-emphasized. We can't really claim to have mastered something until we can recognize and use it out of context.

Not only can your child take the regular SAT's, but today there are SAT Subject Tests corresponding to Algebra 2 and Pre-Calculus, as well as AP Tests for Calculus if your student goes that far. With the competitive nature of today's college admissions, these should not be overlooked by anyone but the weakest students. If you claim that you have done "A" work in Algebra 2, but don't take the Subject Test, many colleges will wonder why.

## Pre-Calculus

Much of Pre-Calculus is simply a repeat of Algebra 2. This year is a good, solid reinforcement of the previous year, which was pretty hard, with just a couple of new topics thrown in. If your kid can get through Algebra 2, Pre-Calculus should pose no problem. It is pretty similar, maybe even a bit easier because by now he is already used to doing very long, very tricky, very abstract problems.

If your child has taken a good, solid Algebra 2 course then Pre-Calculus may not even be necessary. Alex went straight from Algebra 2 to Calculus with no problems, and I have seen other kids do the same. There *were* a few topics in Trigonometry, like the "Double Angle Formula", that he had to go back and look up, but it was pretty straightforward, and most Calculus texts will review this stuff anyway. Other topics, like "Polar Coordinates," don't even show up in the first year of Calculus. If and when kids do get to the second year of Calculus, they often need to review them anyway.

If you are staying involved at this stage yourself, or if you have a very good and involved math tutor, then skipping Pre-Calculus can be an excellent option for a motivated and bright kid. However, if your kid needs to be completely independent in math this year, then taking a Pre-Calculus course is probably the best option.

Pre-Calculus is a course that usually only college-bound students will be taking. For this reason, it is an excellent idea to take the SAT Subject Test at the end of the year.

## Trigonometry?

Most of us have vague, scary memories of something called Trigonometry, that features an Indian princess called Soh-Cah-Toa! Where does this fit into these courses? Are they not teaching it anymore?

The standard approach these days is to split up the subject of Trigonometry, and teach some of it in Algebra 2, and some in Pre-Calculus. This is not written in stone, however, and it varies from curriculum to curriculum. A very strong Algebra 2 course will cover most, if not all, of the trigonometry that you need. If your Algebra 2 course is a little weaker, you will need to do Trigonometry as part of Pre-Calculus.

You have to be aware of this if you are not following just one curriculum for all your math years. Some Pre-Calculus books will assume some prior Trigonometry experience. Some Algebra 2 books won't get that far. On the other hand, with two different texts, there might be a large amount of overlap.

## Calculus

Calculus is my all-time favorite math course. The problems are interesting and, the concepts are compelling. After a long, hard slog with the nitty-gritty details of advanced algebra, we finally get to the fun stuff!

Kids really do need a good, solid foundation in Algebra 2 to do well in this class. Otherwise they will get stuck on the details.

Calculus is basically two main ideas, the Derivative and the Integral. These are ideas that get applied to lines. The ideas themselves are not too hard, and using them on simple lines is something that most kids can understand pretty easily. What makes Calculus really hard for most kids is applying them to all those crazy, squiggly lines that they only barely understood back in Algebra 2!

My suggested approach is to go through an entire Calculus course *just* working on the simple lines called polynomials (You'll know what they are by the time you get there). The Calculus with polynomials is pretty straightforward, and even struggling calculus students can handle it easily. Using just simple lines, your child will be able to cover almost all of the big ideas of Calculus: the derivative, the integral, volumes of crazy-shaped solids, related rates and more.

Once your child understands the big picture, *then* go back and do the same thing all over again, but now include all the other, more difficult functions. There is so much detail to remember when working with all the other functions, - especially the trigonometry functions, that many students get overwhelmed and lost.

This is the approach I took with Alex. While he was still taking Algebra 2 he started asking me about Calculus. He had heard about it, as the "ultimate" math course, I suppose. I thought about it and decided that he probably *could* understand the main ideas, but that the details of doing it with every function under the sun would be too much for him. So I just taught him what I could with polynomials.

It turned out that you can learn most of calculus with just polynomials, so that's what he did. (Remember, Alex is my "math-eager" child, and that *asking* for Calculus is not very common!)

So we did that, then went back and finished his Algebra 2 course. The following year I started him on AP Calculus – the whole thing. By now I had a lot of Calculus books from my tutoring work, but mostly I just used AP Calculus Review books, along with my favorite video series. I like the review books because they are simple and clear, ~~while many of the textbooks really aren't~~!

This was the year that all my hard work paid off. Alex worked mostly independently this year. He checked his own answers, and tried to figure his mistakes out himself. He was mature enough, and *motivated* enough to progress with minimal prodding. I didn't do all the problems I assigned to him beforehand anymore. However, I still did do any he had trouble with by myself before I sat down to help him. He did still often work in the kitchen while I cooked or cleaned, and we were always talking about Calculus. Not only when he got stuck, but when he found a cool problem, because he knew, – or thought – that I was very interested! No matter how busy I was with anything else, I still made a real effort to connect with him on math whenever the opportunity arose.

Again, if your child is taking Calculus, then he is probably college-bound, and he should definitely take the AP Test.

## Consumer Math

One of my favorite things about homeschooling is that we are free to choose *what* to study, and *how* to study it. These math courses I have been talking about may be way too much math for your child – or they may not be enough! I love the fact that we can tailor our child's education to his needs.

A certain level of math education is necessary for everyone. But to be honest, I think many people can perform as successful, well-functioning adults with just pre-algebra and some geometry. Obviously, the further you go in math, the more insight you will have, but it is not necessary for most practical, everyday skills.

If your kid doesn't need the courses to go forward in his education, and also doesn't *want* to take them, then I wouldn't bother. A better option for a kid like this might be "Consumer Math." Consumer Math teaches practical math as it relates to real-world issues like mortgages and credit cards, and is an often-overlooked option.

As much as I love math, if I had a child who was not destined for college, who perhaps wanted to become a professional dancer instead, I definitely wouldn't push algebra on him. Unless he asked for it. There would be no point. He still *would* need to be comfortable with numbers, no matter what his goals, but he wouldn't necessarily need to be able to graph a function.

In fact, sometimes the less you teach, the more they learn. If you force a kid through Algebra 1, and she takes math no further after that, then she will naturally forget most of it. In the long run, it will probably have been a waste of time. Five years from now it will be as if she hadn't taken it at all.

While I consider algebra interesting in its own right, she may not see it that way. Possibly the only long-term knowledge that she will get out of the course is the fact that math *stinks*! She might be much better served by having her arithmetic reinforced for an extra year or two. Consumer math can be an excellent way to do this, while giving her some real-world skills.

It is great that we have choices. That is why we homeschool!

CHAPTER SEVEN
## INCENTIVES

Recently I taught an Economics class to a bunch of homeschooled high school kids. One day the topic was "Incentives."

Economists believe that everything boils down to incentives, and that to achieve your goals, or to get people to do what you want, you just have to get the incentives right. On the assumption that all parents want their kids to do as well as possible at their schoolwork, while kids generally are not quite as motivated, I asked the kids in the class about their schoolwork incentives. What motivated them to do their schoolwork? What made them sit down to their work? What made them try *hard*?

Each of them had one academic area or another that no-one had to "make" them do. Each had something that they enjoyed so much that they pursued it independently. For a couple of the boys it was robotics. Others loved literature or history. For one girl it was classical music. But in this group, math was nobody's favorite. It is amazing how a kid can work so hard, so happily, even obsessively at something that some of us parents might consider to be just as hard or "boring" as math, yet actual math, which we think of as far more important, gets completely neglected!

*How to Homeschool Math - Even if you Hate Fractions!!*

When it came to math, this was a pretty typical group of teens: bright, but somewhat more interested in texting their friends than studying. Most of the kids agreed that they did suffer negative consequences like parental nagging if they neglected their math. However, none of them could describe any *positive* incentives they had for doing it, let alone for doing it well. When I asked if any of them enjoyed "math for math's sake," they laughed out loud!

So I posed the question: "What if you got paid by the hour to do your math?" Cheers and applause all around! They all really liked that idea, of course. However, they pretty quickly admitted that they would probably just go up to their rooms and goof off, while *pretending* to do math! They decided that it probably wouldn't be effective at all.

So I posed the question: "What if your parents gave you $10 for every math assignment you did *well* on?" They thought this would definitely be more effective in general, but individually they weren't convinced that it was worth the effort.

"What if instead of $10, you got $100 for each well-done assignment?"

"I'd be a genius!"

This was Bob, a typical teenage slacker whose mom just pulls her hair out trying to motivate him. Funny thing - I do believe him!

Now, most of us can't or won't give our kids $100 each time they do a good job, because it's ridiculous! But this does illustrate an important point. Even the most math-resistant kid can be motivated by the proper incentive!

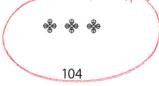

*Chapter Seven: Incentives*

Believe it or not, many kids actually have a motivation to do *poorly* at math. Neither they nor their parents are aware of it, but a powerful de-motivator is at play in some families. Some parents, no matter what their child's level of skill, will *always push for more.* It is never enough for them. If their child is bad at something, they have to be good. If they are good at something, then they have to be great. It is a parenting style rooted in the belief that kids, as a rule, aren't motivated enough. Kids of this type of parents quickly learn not to bother. No matter how well they do, they are still going to get pressed to do *better.* Many of these kids figure, often subconsciously, that if trying hard makes no difference, they might as well put in minimal effort in the first place.

Some parents believe their *job* is to push their children to achieve. Some just get into the habit. This can be fine. All kids really do need a push now and then. The problem comes when parents are always pushing, no matter *what.*

Melissa has been a student of mine for several years, ever since she was in middle school. Her parents are determined that their kids do well in math. Melissa was an average and happy math student in elementary school, but her parents felt that if she really tried she could get into the honors track.

So they hired me and Melissa tried harder. She did do pretty well, and she got into that honors math class. But *now* her parents felt that, if she really tried, she could get an "A" in that class, instead of the "B" she was getting. They were now on her case *all the time*, telling her that she should do more, and do it better. Now she had to see me *twice* a week! By trying to please her parents and getting herself into the honors class, she had actually made things worse for herself. Now the pressure was really on.

From her parents' point of view, their nagging worked. They had actual proof of it! It got her into that honor's class didn't it? If it worked well before, why not now? And now? They had seen their nagging get results, so it became Standard Operating Procedure in their home. Eventually they were afraid that without constant nagging, Melissa would do nothing. So they kept it up, all the time, just to be "safe."

That honors math class was pretty hard for Melissa. However, the constant pressure from her parents made it even harder. Her attitude slipped, along with her grades. She felt like her parents only ever saw her mistakes. She didn't do very well in the class, and went back to the regular math class the following year. The nagging-level from her parents was *no* different, but at least the math was easier!

You would think that with demanding parents like hers, Melissa would be incentivized to do well. That *would* be true if they were content when she reached their goals. But they weren't. Their nagging level was the same, if not *worse*, when she did well. She probably secretly fears that if she actually *were* an A honors student, that the expectations would be raised even higher than that.

Melissa is actually dis-incentivized to do well at math. The better she does, the more is expected of her. The constant message is "You could be better." If you are going to hear that all the time, no matter what, then what's the point of trying hard? This is as true for homeschoolers as it is for school kids!

## It's just *so* Hard to get him to do his Math!

Your child probably gets consequences if he doesn't sit down to do his work. However, he probably won't be in as much trouble if he has a good excuse, rather than admitting to you that he simply didn't *feel like* doing it. He is incentivized to make up an excuse for why he couldn't do it, rather than saying he doesn't want to do it.

See these excuses and procrastination for what they are. If your kid is constantly "forgetting," or too busy, he is actually refusing, but in a nice, polite, un-punishable way!

So why would he refuse? Why do kids hate math? Mostly I hear that it is boring and useless. The useless thing is just a cop-out. They are hoping that we will see their point, agree with them, and decide they don't need to do math anymore! Ha! I am sure that you can think of at least twenty *completely* "useless" activities that your kids participate in eagerly. Point this out to them, however, and they will just tell you, "But this is different!"

The boring thing, now that's a real issue. I put off boring chores all the time, and my massive laundry pile can attest to that. Because laundry bores me, I put it off until I am forced into it by necessity. Bills and dishes tend to fall into this category too, unfortunately. Grown-ups have a hard enough time doing tedious things. If you are expecting your *child* to go off by herself and do something pretty boring, of her own accord, with no immediate, tangible reward, you are dreaming! She will need an incentive.

Economists think money is the number one ideal incentive. Hit people in their pocketbooks and you will change their behavior pretty quickly. However, economists also admit that effective incentives vary from person to person, and that anything that makes us feel good, or brings us any kind of pleasure, can be a powerful incentive.

The positives of sitting down to work at math and *trying*, have to out-weigh the negatives. The negatives associated with math tend to be its "boringness", the isolation, as well as the horrible feelings of frustration and inadequacy!

For many kids there is nothing balancing these out. That is why they hate math.

Math is hard to enforce and incentivize because not only do our children have to sit down to work (easy enough to enforce), they also have to decide to turn their brains on and *think*! (Not so easy to enforce.) We can order them to go do their math. That's easy. If they don't, they don't get to go to the beach. However, ordering them to *think* is next to impossible! How do we know? When he makes a mistake, it is not always clear whether it was a genuine mistake, or whether he just couldn't care less and was sloppy.

Are we going to punish him for every mistake? That doesn't seem reasonable. On the other hand, are we always going to let it go, and allow him to do math only half "awake?" This is tricky. This is why incentives are so important. Concrete, visible actions can have concrete, visible consequences. But thinking? Trying hard? How on earth can we insist on that?

The problem is that we can't force them to think. They have to *want* to. They have to get something out of it, right here, right now!

## Your Attention – the Best Incentive of All!

When we take our math Full-Contact with our kids, we are providing a huge incentive to them. At a young age, there really is nothing they want more than our time and attention. They will do addition if it means doing it with us.

For most young kids, the *only* incentive they need is your loving, positive attention and time. Actually, this is often enough incentive for kids at any age! Do not under-

*Chapter Seven: Incentives*

estimate how powerful this is, even for your hairy, 6ft. teenager!

Many parents expect their kids to be motivated to do well at math by the prospect of getting into college. Unfortunately, for most kids this is way too abstract and far off to make any real difference. I have only seen this incentive really work on juniors and seniors in high school who have already started visiting schools.

Unfortunately, by then, it is often too late. If you want to use the college thing as a motivator, I suggest actually visiting some colleges, and taking some tours. Light that fire in his belly. Otherwise it is too abstract, and it just won't work.

Praise and kudos work are great motivators for kids at any age. They are great incentives! Praise for a problem well solved, or simply for *effort* goes a long way. Let them "catch" you bragging to your friends and family. Tell them how much better *they* are than *you* were at that age. This is powerful stuff! Just beware to not give them an overinflated sense of their abilities that will someday lead to crushing disappointment.

"Hold on a minute!" you may say. "Shouldn't our kids try hard purely for the satisfaction of it? Shouldn't they do well at their subject just from a pure love of it?" Unfortunately, *that* is as likely to happen as them always sharing their candy just because it's the right thing to do! It is a very nice, very unrealistic notion.

Only when your child has mastered some math fundamentals, can you truly expect him to enthusiastically put his games aside and do his math without prompting. Also, the fundamentals of math take a long time to master. Even Alex, who definitely "loves math" would almost always rather go play soccer, tennis, ski or just goof around with his friends! This has changed somewhat as he has gotten older and the math has gotten more compelling, but it's still true more often than not. Forget the idea of the love of math itself being enough of a motivator. Even with a math-loving kid, this only shows up in random bursts. And when it does, it is selectively applied, and only gets directed toward certain types of problems, and not necessarily the ones he's supposed to be working on.

## Show me the Money!

Now, many of you are going to gasp in horror at this, but I am all for cash rewards!

Just like Bob in the story above, most kids really *will* try harder if they are motivated by a cash reward. Yes, they are doing it for the love of money, and not for the pure joy of learning – but they are *doing* it!

Money is an excellent way to turn around a kid whom you consider to be capable but not trying hard enough. Perhaps on her exercise sets she is getting only five out of every ten, and you think she's not really trying. You think that if she *did* try she could definitely get eight or nine right. What you might try then is to tell her that every time she gets eight or more right, per set, you'll give her a cash reward. This motivates her to not only sit down to her work, but also to try! Your reward level should be high enough that she really has to focus to achieve it, but low enough that with effort, she really can achieve it.

I used this approach with Alex when he was 12. It was when he was prepping for the SAT's, and it was the first time he was going off and doing problem sets alone, to practice. The problem sets took him about a half an hour, which was a long time for him.

Even Alex, who loves math, would have rather been playing pretty much anything than sitting there for a half hour doing math problems. If he had to choose among his school subjects he'd choose math every time, but he certainly wouldn't have chosen it over soccer. Not at 12!

I wanted him to do these half-hour practice sets, and I wanted him to do them enthusiastically with his brain turned on. So I told him that I would give him $5 for every problem set where he got more than 75% of the problems correct.

For Alex, at that time, with that book, 75% of those problems was achievable, but not without effort. Being 12, he though $5 each time was *awesome*, and since there were about 15 sets of them in his book, he made some good money!

He got the money most of the time but not *always*, so 75% was a good level to set the reward at. I had given him several similar practice sets before I came up with this scheme, so I knew that my expectations were reasonable. Having a score limit was important, because if I had just given him $5 for every set he *completed*, he would have been motivated to just rush through quickly.

As I mentioned before, I didn't insist that he take the actual SAT test. As the date got closer, it became clear that he actually could do a pretty respectable job, and he was pretty sure he wanted to take the test. To motivate him just a little bit more I told him that if he got over a 550 on the math section I'd give him $200. That was like winning the lottery to him. He could buy an awesome airsoft gun with that! I picked that score because I knew it was fairly reachable. That definitely did motivate him more. While he never *did* go off and study on his own, or do anything <u>completely unrealistic</u> like that, he was pretty agreeable and enthusiastic when I would quiz him on his math facts.

This financially-motivated SAT prep was done over just a 3-month period. I haven't used the money incentive on him since then, even though he has, at times, worked much, much harder. It just seemed like the right thing to do at the time.

He did earn that $200, and I was happy to pay it!

That money gave him a tangible, physical, immediate reward for his efforts, which gave him a little extra motivation and *staying power.*

I have suggested this tactic to other parents, and I have seen it used both effectively and ineffectively. First, the money has to be an "Oh, my gosh!" amount. If I tried to give Alex $5 for anything now, he'd just laugh at me! Second, what you are asking for in return has to be reasonable and within reach.

This tactic is very effective in turning around an unwilling, yet capable student. One student of mine, Deborah, was definitely smart but unwilling. She was the queen of procrastination! If she was ever actually cornered and forced to sit at her books she just turned her brain right off. If she couldn't see the answer immediately she didn't bother. She "forgot" everything – by which I mean she *rejected* everything, because she just didn't want to do it.

She was really smart. She just couldn't be bothered to put any effort into math because she got absolutely nothing out of it. In fact, she got *less* than nothing out of it. Time spent doing math was time that that *wasn't* spent Facebooking with her friends!

Her mother decided to try a drastic financial incentive similar to the one I used with Alex. She promised to give Deborah a cash reward every time she got 80% or more of her problems correct. I must say, Deborah's "Oh, my gosh!" dollar amount was *much* higher than Alex's had been. I could probably go on vacation with what that girl earned! But her reward *had* to be high, in order for it to be effective. It had to be high enough to make Deborah really, *really* want to do it.

And it worked. It worked really, really well. It worked better than her mom expected. Not only did Deborah start to really master the math she was working on, but she started to enjoy it too. The money incentive had caused her to turn her brain on and really think. By doing this she started solving some tricky problems, which made her feel really smart and good about herself. She started to see herself as really good at math. She was starting to accumulate "solved problems," and had some "math victories" under her belt, which increased her academic self-esteem.

Deborah had initially been motivated by the money, but came to really enjoy the math. By the time she grew out of that pre-teen, drama-queen phase, she didn't need that motivation anymore. Thank goodness, because her mom had no money left! (Actually, her mom claims that it was the best money ever spent, and that she'd do it again in a heartbeat.)

We obviously don't want to do this all the time, but it can be an effective short-term tool for some families.

## Eliminate the Negatives & Add the Positives

The negatives of math are the boredom, the isolation, the frustration and the feelings of inadequacy. These have to be neutralized. We can reduce the negative impact by eliminating, or at least reducing, those factors. Adding positive incentives, like praise, attention and rewards works too. Used together, these approaches can turn your whole math experience around.

The suggestions in this book focus on both adding positive incentives as well as reducing negative incentives. The "boring" issue will be improved since you will no longer be assigning pages of rote work for your child to do. This limit on how much work he does will be nicely enforced by the fact that you yourself are going to be sitting with him the whole time he works, and you don't have endless hours to do that. Your sitting with him, in turn, reduces the negative isolation factor for him. His frustration will also be minimized because you will now be prepared, having previously worked through all the problems you are giving him. By being involved this way, identifying and filling in gaps in his knowledge, building a strong foundation and not putting him in a course that is too hard for him, you will also be minimizing any feeling of inadequacy that he may have.

We have to figure out how to incentivize our kids to try hard at their math, and stop trying to force it upon them. It is so much easier when they are willing! By minimizing the negatives, and maximizing the positives we can motivate our kids to really *try*. And trying is the essential ingredient for success.

Full-Contact math eliminates the negative incentives of tedium, isolation and frustration, while also adding the huge positive incentive of parental attention. By taking away the negatives as well as adding positive incentives, we can turn our child's whole math experience around.

CHAPTER EIGHT
# HOPE & MOTIVATION

So, you've read the book, you like the ideas, you see why they might work. There's just one problem: Your child doesn't <u>want</u> to sit and do math with you!

So what do you do then? What if math has become such a contentious topic that you and she just get frustrated at each other? How then, do you take it Full-Contact?

One option is to simply have your spouse take over the math education. If your spouse has the time, the inclination, and the temperament, then this might be the ideal solution. However, this very frequently is not an option, and besides, this won't heal the math rift that has developed between you and your child.

If your child doesn't want to sit with you to do math, you first have to figure out why. Be honest with yourself. Look at your part in it, not *hers*.

Have you been too critical? Too unrealistic in your expectations? Have you gotten frustrated and blown your top at her? Do you drone on and on at her, with her having no idea what you are talking about? Do you tell her directly – or indirectly – that she is no good at math? Lazy? Do you find it hard to find time to sit with her, so that when you finally do, you go on for much longer than you should? Do you seem arbitrary about math – one day it's important, the next it's not? All of these things are common. Any of them can turn your kid off to doing math – especially with you!

Figuring out what you've been doing to turn her off is the big First Step. Forget about *her* part in it. Yes, she's probably been sulky, lazy and rude, but let's just assume that's a symptom, and not a cause. If you can honestly assess what your part has been, then you can start to think about how to do things differently.

Joanna was a busy homeschool mom of three great kids, ages 12, 10 and 8. When she found out that I was a math tutor, she started telling me all of her math woes. "I've just ruined it for Lillian," she confided in me. "The younger two, they're fine, they really like math. But Lillian, Lillian I've *ruined* for math!"

Joanna told me that she had been so hard on Lillian for those first few years of home schooling – so critical, demanding and impatient, that now Lillian just hated math. Every time they would sit together to do math, it ended in a fight. Joanna would get impatient with Lillian; Lillian would get frustrated by her mom. Unkind things were said; feelings were hurt. Usually someone started crying. In fact, it had become such a contentious topic that they hadn't done any math in almost a year!

Lillian now refused to do math with her mother, saying she'd rather work on her own. That would be fine, her mother supposed, but unfortunately Lillian never actually did sit down to math. She had excuse after excuse. "Reasons," she called them. Joanna was wracked with guilt. She knew that she had been too hard on Lillian. She knew that it was she herself who had turned Lillian off to math! It was done, and Joanna had no idea how to undo it.

## Chapter Eight: Hope & Motivation

Guilt is a killer emotion. I don't know one parent who doesn't have guilt about something. None of us is perfect, and we have all messed up plenty of times. But we should remember that we homeschool parents are, by definition, extremely devoted. If we didn't care, we wouldn't bother with all this. For the vast majority of us, life would be "easier" if our kids went to school each day!

Precisely because we *do* care so much, guilt about having "messed up" something relating to our child's education can be overwhelming. Think of all those nay-sayers out there who have just been waiting for a chance to say, "I told you so!"

Honestly, you really *may* be the reason your kid hates math. OK! Whew! Let's just put it out there. Let's stare it straight in the face! So your kid hates math because you've been a yeller, or condescending, or impatient. Or all of the above! For some reason, you thought it was going to be effective. Or you didn't know *what* else to do. But you do love your child. You know it, she knows it, and all the other aspects of your relationship are great. You want to heal your math relationship and help her succeed at math. You wouldn't have bought this book otherwise. Well here's the Good News: <u>Even if your kid is already 16 and still can barely multiply, it is absolutely *not* too late to fix this math thing!</u>

My heart went out to Joanna when she was telling me about Lillian. Joanna was so convinced that she had completely ruined any chance Lillian had of getting a decent math education. She was at her wits' end. At one point Joanna had even hired a tutor, thinking that might help, but the math-fighting between her and Lillian still went on during the week. Now they were fighting over the homework assignments. When tutoring didn't work either, Joanna had all but given up.

"Maybe you should just start over," I suggested.

Joanna and I talked some more about how to possibly turn things around for Lillian, and then Joanna spent some weeks being introspective. When she was really sure that she could be different with Lillian, and also that she had *time* to work with her consistently, and follow the suggestions I outline in this book, she sat Lillian down for a long talk.

Mostly, Joanna apologized. She apologized for being so demanding and unrealistic for all those years. She apologized for having had unrealistic expectations, and for getting frustrated so frequently. She tried to impress upon Lillian that she was absolutely not bad at math, but that instead it was Joanna who had not been an effective teacher for her.

Joanna took *all* the responsibility for the negativity and tension that had sprung up between them regarding math. She owned up to all her "mistakes." This, of course, cleared the air quickly and completely. In the face of an honest, sincere apology, defiance usually washes right away.

I was quite impressed by Joanna's humble apology. However, Joanna dismissed my admiration by pointing out that she really hadn't told her daughter anything she hadn't already known! "This was not news to her," Joanna said. "What *was* new, was hearing me *admit* it!"

After her apology, Joanna told Lillian that she wanted to try again. She proposed going back to the very beginning math topics together, taking their time, and just seeing what happened. No rush, no pressure. Lillian agreed.

Going back to the beginning math topics was an excellent idea for two reasons. First, when math is learned in a contentious and stressful atmosphere, it is not learned well.

## Chapter Eight: Hope & Motivation

There were definite gaps in Lillian's math knowledge, and these absolutely needed to be filled in.

Second, going back to the beginning topics meant that most of the stuff they were covering was relatively easy. That helped make these first sessions more relaxing and enjoyable, and gave Joanna lots of opportunities to be positive and affirming.

Joanna applied all the suggestions from this book. In the past, Joanna had always been one of those-on-the-spot helpers: When Lillian needed help Joanna would swoop in, sit down and try to solve the problem then and there. Before she was done, Joanna had often confused Lillian more than ever. This time Joanna made sure that she knew how to do each and every problem she assigned to Lillian before she sat down with her. When Lillian needed help, Joanna was ready, with a quick, clear explanation.

Joanna worked hard at re-building Lillian's confidence and made a conscious effort to give abundant, *authentic* praise. She also worked at making it a nice time for the two of them. Some days they went to the library, then out for ice-cream. Many days Lillian's siblings would have to go and keep themselves busy while Lillian got 100%, one-on-one attention, which made her feel special and important.

Joanna also made time for math every day. She kept the sessions short and sweet, and quit before either one of them became tired or frustrated. And most of all, she resisted the urge to jump ahead. She had the patience to go back to the beginning, to go at Lillian's pace and she resisted the urge to try to catch up too quickly. No matter how much pressure she *herself* felt on that front, she didn't let it show, and she forced herself to take as long as was needed.

Of course, Lillian hadn't trusted this "new" math mom right away. She had had some reservations. But Joanna was true to her word. She never again lost her temper or even showed frustration during their math sessions. It has been almost a year since then, and even though Lillian is not quite at grade-level, she is catching up quickly, and more importantly, she is enjoying it!

Whatever you may have done to turn your child off to math, you can definitely turn it around. All it takes is an honest assessment of the situation, and a willingness to try a new approach.

The apology doesn't have to be a groveling, "I'm the worst parent *ever!*" type of thing. You can say simply that you were inexperienced, and that you didn't know then what you know now, and that you'd like to try a different approach.

Or you can simply say nothing and just jump in and start teaching math Full-Contact. She might be a little puzzled at first, and somewhat resistant, but very quickly you will win her over, I promise!

Don't try to get an equal-but-opposite apology from *her.* Don't try to get her to admit she was lazy. She probably *was*, but let's just assume that it came from lack of motivation and negative feelings. I'm sure she is not *inherently* lazy. Very few people really are.

Whatever your child's age, it is not too late to start again. If your child is on the older side, you will have to resist the strong urge to "catch up quickly." Take the time, go back and review. No matter how panicked *you* may feel about how behind he is, do not let it show! Your child needs as little emotional stress around math as possible. If you consistently follow the suggestions in this book, by taking it Full-Contact, brushing up, and being prepared, you will progress faster than you might think. Relax – or at least *pretend* to relax!

Be aware, though, – you may have to be extra patient for a while. <u>It is a *lot* harder to *undo* confusion and negativity</u> than it is to learn something clearly and positively in the first place.

Say, for example, that percents are something she always struggled with. You are going to have to go slower, be more prepared yourself, and have even more patience than if she had never even *heard* of percents before.

If there has been anger and frustration around this topic in the past, then that will be "noise" in her head when she does it again with you now. It is very, very hard to concentrate and learn when you have the "I'm a failure" song stuck in your head on repeat. Math as a whole, and this topic in particular, will have to lose its negative associations before it can get fully mastered. That can take some time.

Videos can be a great tool in this type of situation. Get a video series and watch it *together*. Do the exercises *together*. That way <u>you</u> are not the teacher! In fact, you are both students, – in it together.

If she still can't understand a topic, after using a couple different resources, then see if you can't put it off for a while. Sometimes that happens when a kid has been previously very confused or upset about a topic. They just believe that they don't get it, so they don't. However you *really* feel about it, just tell her that it is no problem, and that you are sure she'll get it later. Then continue to put other math in front of her that she will have success with. This will build up her confidence, and start to quiet the noise in her head.

Then, on your own time, you can think more about how to explain the troubling topic in a way that she will understand.

No matter how late you think it is, you *can* fix this. Don't let guilt keep you in denial and prevent you from jumping back in, armed with a new positive attitude and a new approach!

## ... and Motivation

This math thing is a lot of work, I'm not going to lie. But if you were afraid of hard work, you wouldn't be a homeschool parent in the first place!

In this last section I will share my own personal, favorite reasons for why our kids all need solid math skills. However, please don't turn around and lecture your child with these reasons, in order to motivate him. I'll tell you right now that it won't work. These reasons are for *you*. Reflect on them yourself as a way to motivate *you*.

Some of our kids will homeschool high school and then go straight to work. If your child wants to be a construction worker, dog trainer, dancer or writer, he still needs decent arithmetic skills. He may not need them for his daily work, but he will still need them for his everyday life. To manage his credit cards, buy a home, manage his budget, and more importantly, to not get *conned*.

He will need to compare one deal to another, and know for sure which is better. He will need to be comfortable enough with numbers and have a confident attitude toward them, so that he can live his life making informed decisions. Many skilled workers work for themselves, in their own small businesses, or as contractors. Working for oneself takes good number sense. These businesses are often too small to afford bookkeepers – he will have to do it for himself. There are budgets, invoices, bills – and taxes! Without a positive attitude toward numbers and a solid mastery of arithmetic, these tasks will be a constant challenge.

Even if your daughter is destined to be "just" (Ha!) a homemaker, arithmetic skills and math confidence will be invaluable. What if she marries someone who can't add two plus two? How are they going to buy a home, do their taxes or manage their finances? If math is a scary topic for her, these things will be pretty challenging. On the other hand, what if she marries a "math-savvy"' guy? If she herself is math-illiterate, she will be at the mercy of his judgment in most of the major decisions in their lives.

On the subject of our daughters. I think it is especially important that mothers-of-daughters be the parent to jump in and be the hands-on math teacher. In spite of today's modern society, most of the homeschool families I see are single-worker households, with Dad being the one who works. We may all be broke without that second income, but this is the norm in our communities! Some of the moms are working part time, and in this economy, some of the dads are unemployed while the moms work, but overwhelmingly it is mom who stays home, who raises and homeschools the kids.

Girls frequently aspire to live a life similar to their mother's. If mom uses no math in her life, she won't be too convincing when she tells her daughter that math is a very important skill. If Mom doesn't remember her own schoolday math, or worse, doesn't show any *interest* in it, she is communicating loud and clear. She may be telling her daughter that math is important, but she is demonstrating that it is not. Not for *her*, at least! And so, by association, not for her daughter.

Mom will be a lot more convincing if she herself is the one to brush up on her math skills and do the teaching. Then Mom is demonstrating that math skills are important even in her own "Homeschool Mom Life." This is the life her daughter may secretly or subconsciously aspire to, even if she *says* that she wants to be a doctor. In fact, maybe the best reason for our girls to have serious and solid math skills is so that they can be homeschool mothers themselves, and pass their skills on to the next generation.

In today's world most girls are not being raised to be home-makers primarily. We parents nowadays have a bigger vision for them. We want them to see that they have choices, and to feel that they can do anything a man can do. They don't need to depend on a man; they can be self-sufficient!

Many of us send our daughters to girls' empowerment groups, girls'-this and girls'-that. When we study history, we emphasize the roles of women. We pick literature that has female heroines, and positive, empowering messages. Yet math? Well, we're not *that* liberated!

If you *truly* want your daughter to grow up to be a strong female warrior, then do her a favor. Give her a weapon she can really use: <u>give her math</u>!

## Chapter Eight: Hope & Motivation

For many of us, the primary reason we want our kids to learn math is so that they can get into a decent college. Obviously, if our kids want to go on to any form of higher education, a solid math foundation is essential. This we all know. Colleges are more competitive than ever, and high scores on standardized tests are a requirement for most of the top schools.

If your child wants to become an engineer or scientist, it's obvious that he will need the best possible math skills. But what if he wants to be a historian?

College is not what it used to be. It is no longer a ticket to the middle class. Many fields today require a master's degree, or more. Many people assume that if their child wants to study a field in the humanities, he won't need advanced math skills. Unfortunately, that is only true if he doesn't want to go very far in his field!

If your child really does want to become a historian, then he will absolutely have to have a serious and solid math foundation. Historians frequently have to work with and understand statistics. If a historian doesn't understand statistics, how will he be able to interpret data or do research? He will be at the mercy of other people's interpretations of historical data. When it comes time to write his Thesis, he will probably need a working knowledge of Statistics. That may not seem like a big deal, until you realize that serious Statistics courses are taught *after* Calculus!

This is true in many of the fields that people generally don't think of as requiring "good" math skills. Psychology, Anthropology, Sociology, Education and more. Math skills may not come into play in the first few years of study in these fields, but they absolutely will.

Another reason to learn math, touched on in Chapter 3, is for the purely aesthetic value of it. Far less practical than personal finances or the pursuit of higher education, is the study of math purely as an *art*. Art for art's sake is a worthy pursuit.

My last, and favorite, reason that a solid math education is so important, is that it enables us to be well-informed citizens. No matter what your child's career aspirations are, to be a well-educated and informed citizen and to vote knowledgably and responsibly, he needs to understand math. Without mathematical understanding, he will never be able to truly understand what is being said, or implied, on the evening news!

"Positives and negatives" is a huge stumbling block for arithmetic students. What the heck does it mean to "subtract a negative number" anyway? If he can't get that, then the daily news will be too much. Listen closely to the news and you will hear phrases like "negative growth." It's the same idea, and we need to understand it to know our world. When we don't understand the topics on the news, we tend to just tune it out, and tell ourselves that we are "not interested."

The news is littered with phrases that go right over our heads or get misunderstood unless we understand math. What does it really mean for the population to be growing exponentially? Or for the increase in car prices to be 1.2%?

If there is one good reason for every one of us to have a decent mathematical education, it is so that we can understand economics. The world is so complicated today that

## Chapter Eight: Hope & Motivation

without a basic knowledge of economics we can't really begin to understand it. Understanding economics is essential to understanding Politics, Global Affairs, History, and even Human Nature!

And understanding math is *essential* to understanding economics.

So to understand politics, you need to understand math! To understand history you need to understand math. To und...you get my point. This is why Algebra 2 is generally a requirement for high school graduation. The details may never get used again, but the *ideas* certainly will.

Calculus too, helps us to understand the world around us, and to become well-educated, well-informed citizens. Calculus is all about rates of change. And then about the rate of those *rates* changing! It is pretty crazy stuff – but very real-world. When the news anchors say that "Job Growth is Decreasing" they don't mean that the number of jobs is going down. They really mean that it is not going up as fast as it used to. The actual number of jobs is still increasing! Spend a year on Calculus and that stuff becomes clear. Otherwise, you might easily be fooled by a clever politician into thinking that people are actually *losing* their jobs.

## Don't get fooled – *get math!*

## ACKNOWLEDGEMENTS

I would like to thank Lockey Coughlin for her tireless support and enthusiasm for this project. Also, I would like to thank my editor Marc Sichel for all his great suggestions. Lastly, I would like to thank all my students and their families who have shared so much with me, and given me the insights presented in this book.

APPENDIX

# THE SEQUENCE OF TOPICS

Many parents get confused as to exactly *what* math their child should be learning at any given point. Every book seems to introduce different topics at different times in different ways. Unless you use one single curriculum from beginning to end, it can be really easy to have gaps in your math knowledge.

This chapter includes the major math topics in the general order they should be mastered. This is not meant to be used as a complete or comprehensive list, but rather as a *guide*. This list starts with basic arithmetic and covers the main topics up through Pre-Calculus.

You can use this list to determine what skills your child should already have, given what she is currently studying. Not having mastered the pre-requisites can be a recipe for disaster at any level. This list can be used to make sure that your child's math foundation is strong.

You can also simply follow this sequence of topics, studying them as you wish. You can switch textbooks and resources as you see fit. This is what I did. I went topic to

*How to Homeschool Math - Even if you Hate Fractions!!*

topic, using several resources at each stop. I was less concerned with whether the topic was Pre-Algebra or Algebra 1, than whether it was the logically next, right thing. to learn

You may not know what I mean by some of these topics. That's fine. Nothing listed here is obscure, or outside the mainstream, so you will be able to look them up. There are lots of excellent books out there that will explain these topics much better than I could ever hope to!

### ***Notes:***

*I have listed the Geometry topics before Algebra, but they can be covered later or simultaneously, if you like.*

+   indicates topics that are frequently not covered well enough: Pay extra attention!

\#   indicates standalone topics within a course.

*Appendix*

## ARITHMETIC

1. The Number Line
2. Place Value
3. Whole numbers
    - Add/subtract/multiply/divide
4. Decimals
    - Add/subtract/multiply/divide
5. Fractions +
    - Add/subtract/multiply/divide
    - Mixed numbers/Improper Fractions
    - Equivalent Fractions
6. Percents
    - What exactly is a percent?
    - Find a given percent of a number
    - Converting between percent/fraction/decimal equivalents
7. Order of Operations
8. Factors and Multiples
9. Prime Factorization
10. Definitions: Factor, Multiple
11. Arithmetic with Negative Numbers +
    - Adding and subtracting
    - Multiplying and Dividing
12. Word problems involving all of these skills

## PRE-ALGEBRA

1. More Percents:
   - Find a certain % of a number
   - Find what % one number is of another
   - Find Percent Increase
   - Word problems
2. Simple Probabilities
3. Intro to the Coordinate grid
   - Plot points
   - What are the coordinates of a given point?
4. Mean, Median & Mode #
5. Bar and Pie graphs #
6. Venn Diagrams #
7. Sales tax, commission, discounts, profits #
8. Unit Conversions
9. Squares and square roots
10. Geometry basics
    - Shapes
    - Perimeter
    - Area
    - Pythagorean Theorem
    - Surface area
    - Volume
11. Simple equations – one variable
    - Word Problems
12. Simple equations – two variables
    - Substitution method only
    - Word Problems
13. Ratios and Proportions +
14. Inequalities
    - Recognize the symbols
    - Use in an equation

15. Scientific Notation #
16. Simple and compound interest #
17. Exponents

# GEOMETRY

1. All basic angle, line and area facts about
   - Triangles
   - Squares, Rectangles, Parallelograms
   - Kites, Rhombus
   - Circles
   - General Polygons
2. Parallel Lines and Transversals
3. Sum of degrees
   - In Triangles
   - In Other polygons
   - Around a point
   - Making a straight line
4. Triangle types and their properties
5. Right Triangles
   - Pythagorean Theorem
   - Special Right Triangles
6. Congruent Triangles
7. Surface area and Volume of Solids
   - Cylinders/Prisms
   - Cones/Pyramids
8. Coordinate Geometry
   - Transformations
   - Distance between two points
   - Midpoint
9. Lots of problems using all these facts in combination

Appendix

# ALGEBRA 1 AND 2

1. Solving Equations with 1 variable
2. Solving Equations with 2 variables
    - Substitution
    - Elimination
3. Graphing Linear Equations with 2 variables
    - Graph equation by plugging in values
    - Graph by using: $y = mx+b$
        i. What is Slope?
        ii. What is Y-Intercept?
        iii. Rewrite equations in various formats
            1. Slope-intercept
            2. Point-slope
            3. Standard
    - Interpret graph to create the equation
    - Write the equation given a point and the slope
    - Write the equation given 2 points
4. 2-Equation, 2-Variable Word Problems
    - Consecutive Integer
    - Money
    - Distance/Rate/Time
    - Lever/Pulley
5. Solving and Graphing Inequalities with 1 and 2 variables
6. Arithmetic of Exponents
    - Add/subtract/multiply and divide expressions with exponents in them
    - Understand and use Negative Exponents +
    - Understand and use Fractional Exponents +
7. Arithmetic of Radicals
    - Simplified expressions
    - Rationalized denominator

8. Introduction to The Function +
   - What is it? Why the new notation?
   - What are domain and range?
9. Polynomials
   - What are they?
   - Arithmetic: Add/subtract/multiply ~~and~~ divide polynomial expressions
   - Factoring polynomials
10. Quadratic Functions
    - Quadratic expressions
        i. ~~What are they?~~ Graphing eqn
        ii. ~~Arithmetic: Add/subtract/multiply and divide quadratic expressions~~
        iii. Factoring
        iv. FOIL
    - Quadratic equations
        i. What are they?
        ii. How to solve them/Finding Roots
            1. Factoring
            2. Quadratic formula
            3. Completing the Square
    - Graphing Quadratic Functions
    - Word problems using quadratic equations
11. Higher-Degree Polynomial Functions
    - Polynomial Long division
    - Graph higher-order polynomial functions
    - Finding roots of higher order polynomial functions
12. Rational Functions
    - Rational Expressions
        i. What are they?
        ii. Arithmetic: Add/subtract/multiply and divide quadratic expressions

- Solving Rational Equations
- Graphing Rational Functions
    i. Finding asymptotes
- Word problems using rational equations and functions
13. Absolute Value Functions
    - Solving absolute value equations
    - Graphing Absolute Value Functions
    - Inequalities combined with Absolute value
    - Describe a real-world requirement as an Absolute Value Function
14. Imaginary Numbers #
15. Matrices #
    - Add/subtract/Scalar Multiply
    - Multiply Matrices
    - Use Matrices to solve systems of equations
16. Functions +
    - Be able to work with and understand function notation
    - Add and subtract Functions
    - Composition of functions
17. Inverse Functions
    - What are they?
    - How to determine them
    - Graphing Inverse Functions
18. Exponential Functions
    - What are they?
    - What they model in the real world
    - Graphing them
    - Word Problems
        i. Compound interest
        ii. Bacterial Growth

19. Logarithms
    - What are they?
    - Add/subtract/multiply/divide
    - Change of Base Formula
    - Solving Logarithmic Equations
20. Logarithmic Functions
    - Relationship to exponential function
    - Graphing Logarithmic Functions
21. Arithmetic and Geometric Sequence and Series #
22. Counting #
    - Permutations
    - Combinations
23. Advanced probabilities problems #
24. Transformations of all functions
25. Conic sections
    - Graph and write Equations for
        i. Parabola
        ii. Circle
        iii. Ellipse
        iv. Hyperbola
26. Right Triangle Trigonometry
    - Sin, Cos, Tan
    - Sec, Cos, Cot
    - Inverse Trig Functions
    - Find a side of a right triangle; find an angle
27. The Unit Circle
28. Radians
29. Trigonometric Identities
    - Law of Sines, Law of Cosines
    - Pythagorean Identities
    - Negative Angle Identities
    - Co-function Identities

- Sum and Difference Identities
- Double-Angle, Half-Angle Identities
30. Trigonometric Functions
    - Graphing Trig Functions
    - Transformations of Trig Functions
31. Word Problems, real-world applications of Trig Functions

## PRE-CALCULUS

1. Vectors
   - What are they?
   - Arithmetic of Vectors: add/subtract/scalar multiply
   - The Unit Vector
   - Dot Product
   - Cross-Product
   - Word problems, real-world applications with vectors
2. Parametric Equations
   - What are they?
   - Writing Parametric Equations
3. Polar Coordinates
   - What are they?
   - Plotting points
   - Graphing
   - Converting to and from Cartesian Coordinates
   - Using Polar Coordinates with Complex Numbers

Made in the USA
Charleston, SC
13 October 2011